Seven Stone Steps
Stepping Up to Godliness

DAN MANNINGHAM

Seven Stone Steps
Stepping Up to Godliness
by Dan Manningham

Copyright 2012 © FOCUS PUBLISHING, INC.
All rights reserved.

No part of this book may be reproduced by any means
without written consent of the publisher
except for brief quotes used in reviews written specifically
for use in a magazine or newspaper.

Scripture references are quoted from
The New International Version of the Bible
and where noted,
The King James Version,
The New King James Version,
The New American Standard Bible,
and the English Standard Version.

Cover design by Melanie Schmidt
Cover photograph by Gay Ayers
(www.gayayers.com)
Used by permission

ISBN 978-1885904-94-2

PRINTED IN THE UNITED STATES OF AMERICA
BY
FOCUS PUBLISHING
Bemidji, Minnesota

Dedication

To my beloved Fran
and
to Havac and Lucas
(You know who you are)

Table of Contents

FOREWORD	3
INTRODUCTION	7
CHAPTER ONE Stepping Out in Obedience	15
CHAPTER TWO Stepping Higher in Virtue	27
CHAPTER THREE The Step of Goodness	41
CHAPTER FOUR The Step of Knowledge	51
CHAPTER FIVE The Step of Self-Control	63
CHAPTER SIX The Step of Perseverance	75
CHAPTER SEVEN The Step of Godliness	85
CHAPTER EIGHT The Step of Brotherly Kindness	93
CHAPTER NINE The Step of Love	103
CHAPTER TEN Staying on Track	113

Foreword

"The power of man's virtue should never be measured by his special efforts, but by his ordinary doing."
-Blaise Pascal

**For this very reason, make every effort to add to your faith goodness; and to goodness, knowledge; and to knowledge, self-control; and to self-control, perseverance; and to perseverance, godliness; and to godliness, brotherly kindness; and to brotherly kindness, love.
2 Peter 1:5-7**

This is the third book in what has become an impromptu series best summarized by the four verses of Philippians 4:6-9. It did not start that way, but by the law of unintended results it has become that.

The first book, *Six Stone Jars: God's Remedy for Fear, Worry and Anxiety,* addresses Paul's command to *"not be anxious about anything"* (verse 6).

The second, *Eight Stone Gates: Taking Thoughts Captive,* explores Paul's instruction to *"think about such things"* (verse 8), disciplining our thoughts by concentrating on eight general topics.

This last book examines the meaning of Paul's statement to *"put into practice"* (verse 9) the virtues that he has described in his letters to the churches. And there are many such virtues that Paul and others declare in their letters to the churches, but for various reasons I have elected to build this book around Peter's list of seven virtues in 2 Peter 1:5-8. What does it mean to *"put into practice"* the Godly virtues described by the authors of the Bible?

As we learn to cultivate these Christian virtues, we will use the metaphor of stepping upward, as the Jews of Israel had to do in climbing up the stone steps to the temple, but the application here is for those who consider themselves to be Christians. These are not the virtues that we develop through grit and determination, but those that we acquire by humbly submitting to the presence and power of God within us.

There are several biblical passages that present us with lists of behaviors appropriate for Christians who desire a deeper and more genuine spiritual life. But I like the list that Peter includes in the first chapter of his second epistle. The virtues described there appear, at first reading, to be so general as to be somewhat vague. Goodness? Godliness? Knowledge? What can Peter possibly hope to accomplish with that kind of grandmotherly advice?

On closer inspection, each of these apparently imprecise qualities can be dissected into very pertinent behaviors that together form the matrix of Godly conduct. But, in that regard, there are two things that must be said.

First, we do not (cannot) establish our relationship with God through conduct. That is done by God's inexhaustible grace through our faith. We become children of God and we remain His children by our faith in what He has done on our behalf; by the atoning work of Jesus Christ on the cross; by the sacrifice and blood of the Lamb of God. Then the virtues follow as a response of gratitude and humility and not as a merit system for acceptance. Consider the Prodigal son; the woman taken in the act of adultery, the thief on the cross. Mercy, grace and salvation are completely His work and the fruit of virtuous living is our feeble, thankful response.

Foreword

Second, this is no easy task because we are confronted at every turn with our own weakness and our own need to diligently lean on the strength of God within to foster those very qualities in our own daily lives. In the end we are left with two options. We can ignore the whole matter because it is a theological minefield and because we feel unworthy, which we clearly are. Or, we can choose to plow ahead, despite our obvious inadequacies, in the hopes of improving our own understanding and thereby encouraging our fellow travelers.

As for me, I choose to hitch up the plow because . . .

> **A tree is recognized by its fruit.**
> **Matthew 12:33**

And I am challenged by this admonition . . .

> **Do not merely listen to the word,**
> **and so deceive yourselves.**
> **Do what it says.**
> **James 1:22**

And I know that . . .

> **I can do everything through him**
> **who gives me strength.**
> **Philippians 4:13**

And I remind myself that . . .

> "God does not ask the impossible, but instructs you to do what you are able, and to pray for aid in doing what you are not able to do yourself, that He may help you."
> -Decree of the Council of Trent, 1564

Seven Stone Steps

Because finally . . .

"What good am I if I know and don't do?
If I see and don't say?
If I look right through you?
If I turn a deaf ear to the thundering sky?
What good am I?"
-Bob Dylan

Dan Manningham
Mansfield, OH

Introduction
Seeing the Temple

"If you can be well without health,
you may be happy without virtue."
-Edmund Burke

**For we are the temple of the living God . . .
Therefore come out from them
and be separate, says the Lord.
2 Corinthians 6:16**

The temple of God is a theme that begins very early in the biblical story. In Exodus 29:9 God begins to describe a sort of portable temple, which He calls a "tabernacle" and which He commands the Jewish people to build and maintain. The tabernacle is really a tent and the Hebrew word used has the meaning of a dwelling place—not just a tent but someone's home. It is a lovely and elaborate tent, but it is, nevertheless, a wooden framework draped with material to enclose it, and it is fully transportable.

But while the tabernacle was fundamentally a portable tent, it was extraordinarily important to God. Dutch theologian, Hermann Witsius (1636-1708), noted that:

> "God created the whole world in six days, but he used forty days to instruct Moses about the tabernacle. Little over one chapter was needed to describe the construction of the world, but six chapters were needed to explain the design of the tabernacle."

This tabernacle was magnificently decorated with the finest materials and workmanship available. They included a ton of gold, three tons of silver and two tons of bronze, plus a fortune in jewels and rare, dyed animal skins. Gold, silver, bronze, costly dies, rare animal hides and artistically worked wood and metal were used to create a tent that was beautiful to behold both inside and out (Exodus 38:24-31).

But the really unique thing about this tabernacle was that God Himself promised to dwell there, and for that reason it was holy—holy beyond any other thing on earth. Nothing profane or irreverent or wicked could be allowed in or near the tabernacle. The tabernacle was set apart for God's purposes. It was sanctified. It was nothing less than His home on earth.

Five hundred years later, when Solomon was king, God directed the building of a permanent temple in Jerusalem to replace the tabernacle. It was arguably the most majestic and costly building ever constructed. 153,600 workers labored together with the finest materials available. Modern estimates of its cost exceed $100 billion (1 Chronicles 22:14).

The inside was completely overlaid with pure gold and decorated lavishly with rare jewels. The columns and capitals and stone work were carved and chiseled by the finest craftsmen over years of time. When it was completed and dedicated, God promised that He would be present in that building; that he would personally inhabit the temple; that it would be His residence on earth. Like the tabernacle, the temple was to be diligently maintained in a physical and spiritual state of purity. Nothing sacrilegious or disrespectful could be tolerated. The temple was set apart for God's purposes. It was sanctified. The Tabernacle was no longer needed and was reverently destroyed. The Temple became God's home on earth.

When it was completed in 957 BC, the temple was wondrous for its beauty, both inside and out. From a distance it was dazzling to the eye in the Judean sunlight and on the inside it

Introduction: Seeing the Temple

was furnished and decorated as no other building on earth. It was a place that would attract people with a heart to worship God.

Solomon's temple sat on top of a hill and anyone approaching it would have to climb upwards by way of stone steps in order to reach it. Each step up brought a Jewish believer closer to the very presence of God because God had promised to actually reside there. It was not a symbol. It was the real and authentic dwelling place of God on earth.

But then, the temple was destroyed in 586 BC by the Babylonians and the Jews were dragged away into exile. Jerusalem was destroyed and the Jewish nation was adrift, without the Temple and God's presence but with a deep longing for that to be restored.

Ezekiel was one of those carried off to Babylon. While in Babylon, he prophesied to the other exiles about God's plans and desires for them. In the fortieth chapter of the book that bears his name, God gave Ezekiel a vision of a new temple—a purely visionary temple—that represented the kind of worship and relationship that He desired for His people. As part of that revelation, God showed Ezekiel that the temple's inner court was accessed by seven stone steps. Seven stone steps led up from their shabby and callous daily life to the very presence of God in the inner court. Seven stone steps from lethargy and indifference to God's throne. *"Seven steps led up to . . . the gate to the inner court . . ."* (Ezekiel 40:22).

> "Virtue is a state of war, and to live in it
> we have always to combat ourselves."
> -Jean Jacques Rousseau

**Don't you know that you yourselves are God's
temple and that God's Spirit lives in you?
1 Corinthians 3:16**

Seven Stone Steps

In the New Testament Jesus changed all that. He created an entirely fresh and radical concept of God's temple. No longer would God's presence abide in a tabernacle of animal skins or a temple of limestone. Under this new covenant (new working arrangement), God's presence would reside directly in every individual person who placed his eternal faith and confidence in the salvation and lordship of Jesus Christ. Those who acknowledged that their only hope for an eternal life with God was the atoning work of Jesus Christ would have within themselves the Holy Spirit of God, the third person of the Trinity and fully God Himself. Those believers' bodies would be temples. They were set apart for God's purposes. They, themselves, were sanctified. They were actually and truly God's home on earth. The limestone temple was no longer needed, and it was utterly destroyed by Roman legions in AD 70. By then, God had countless individual temples of flesh.

But even with the personal indwelling presence of the Holy Spirit, the Christ follower is still instructed to climb higher. It is not expressed in any physical way but it is commanded everywhere that we are to mature in our spiritual life through the development of virtues that are suitable to this personal relationship with God, the indwelling God. Several verses in the New Testament describe our goal as becoming "perfect," but the Greek word "teleios" is better translated "mature," "full grown," or "complete." That is our goal in all of this: maturity in all the dimensions of life through the proper exercise of Christian virtues, and always by the power of the Holy Spirit.

Climbing those steps to the temple of Ezekiel's vision is an appropriate illustration for New Testament believers. It is a picture of stepping up in our spiritual lives by embracing the virtues described in Scripture. Cultivating those virtues is one more means to a closer fellowship with God, who has adopted us as His children, because those virtues represent the very character of God Himself. And even adopted children are expected to mature.

Introduction: Seeing the Temple

3000 years ago committed Jews honored God by climbing those stone steps to be closer to Him. Today those steps are represented by the active cultivation of personal virtues which replicate His nature and are thus suitable to our function as a temple of the living God. Consider just a few:

- Love God with all your heart and soul and mind and love other people as yourself (Matthew 22:37).
- Put on compassion, kindness, gentleness, humility and patience (Colossians 3:12-14).
- Confine your thinking to things that are true, noble, right, pure, lovely, admirable, excellent and praiseworthy (Philippians 4:8).
- Be joyful in hope, patient in affliction, faithful in prayer, generous and hospitable (Romans 12:12-13).
- Pursue righteousness, faith, love and peace (2 Timothy 2:22).

All of these we do that we may grow in maturity and please the Father, and not because they make us any more or less His sons and daughters.

In Peter's second letter, he pens a reminder about how and what the believer's relationship with God is.

> **His divine power has given us everything we need for life and godliness through our knowledge of him who called us by his own glory and goodness. Through these he has given us his very great and precious promises, so that through them you may participate in the divine nature and escape the corruption in the world caused by evil desires (2 Peter 1:3-4).**

Seven Stone Steps

Peter begins with a reminder of the great promises that God has made to us—promises that make it possible for us to escape the sordid moral climate that permeates the world and to actually take part in some way in His divine nature. Peter wants us to know that the basis for any efforts at virtue are anchored in the work that has already been accomplished through Jesus Christ rather than some sort of merit system for whatever we might do.

Then, using that introduction as a foundation Peter moves quickly to what we should do about it . . .

> **For this very reason, make every effort to add to your faith <u>goodness</u>; and to goodness, <u>knowledge</u>; and to knowledge, <u>self-control</u>; and to self-control, <u>perseverance</u>; and to perseverance, <u>godliness</u>; and to godliness, <u>brotherly kindness</u>; and to brotherly kindness, <u>love</u> (2 Peter 1:5-7, emphasis mine).**

Finally, Peter concludes this section with an encouragement and a warning.

> **For if you possess these qualities in increasing measure, they will keep you from being ineffective and unproductive in your knowledge of our Lord Jesus Christ. But if anyone does not have them, he is nearsighted and blind, and has forgotten that he has been cleansed from his past sins (2 Peter 1:3:8-9).**

> "We are like plants in mines, which never saw the sun, but dream of him, and guess where he may be, and do the best to climb, and get to him."
> -Robert Browning Hamilton

Introduction: Seeing the Temple

> **... continue to work out your salvation with fear and trembling, for it is God who works in you to will and to act according to his good purpose.**
> **Philippians 2:12b-13**

In the New Testament view of the temple there are no stone steps that carry us closer to God but there are virtues to refine that can be thought of as steps that bring our nature closer to His. These virtues will not change the eternal relationship between God and those He calls His children, but they are the behaviors that the Father finds pleasing and honoring because they are the very virtues that He, Himself, possesses. They are virtues that those who desire to live at a higher level will strive to develop precisely because they want to be more like Him. They are the virtues that most honor the indwelling God and represent Him to a lost world.

It must be quickly noted that these virtues can only be developed through the power of the indwelling Holy Spirit. You cannot tough this out but you can reach for the strength that is offered to those who want it. *"I can do everything through him who gives me strength"* (Philippians 4:13). It is a circular arrangement by which the indwelling Holy Spirit provides the strength and motivation to cultivate the very virtues that are pleasing to God.

Climbing the steps to the temple was a solemn and deliberate act of moving from the coarse and the common into the very presence of God. Developing Godly virtues in our lives moves us from the crass and familiar to the character of God Himself. And while we will never arrive, we can move closer, step higher, grow wiser.

Peter has described seven cardinal virtues to *"add to our faith"* and promises that in so doing we will *"[be kept] from being ineffective and unproductive in your knowledge of our Lord Jesus*

Seven Stone Steps

Christ." And he further admonishes . . . *"If anyone does not have them, he is nearsighted and blind, and has forgotten that he has been cleansed from his past sins."*

It is a serious and hallowed challenge. Stepping up requires courage and determination, but the benefits are great. It is never too late to be more effective and more productive in our knowledge of the Lord Jesus Christ. Think of those seven stone steps. Think of these seven virtues added to your faith. It is never too late to start climbing.

> "Every day you may make progress.
> Every step may be fruitful. Yet there will
> stretch out before you an ever-lengthening,
> ever-ascending, ever-improving path.
> You know you will never get to
> the end of the journey.
> But this, so far from discouraging, only adds
> to the joy and glory of the climb."
> -Winston Churchill

**Whether you turn to the right or to the left,
your ears will hear a voice behind you, saying,
"This is the way; walk in it."
Isaiah 30:21**

Chapter One

Stepping Out in Obedience

"Rest in this—It is His business to lead, command, impel, send, call . . . It is your business to obey, follow, move, respond . . . ."
-Jim Elliot

**Lord, we show our trust in you by obeying your laws; our heart's desire is to glorify your name.
Isaiah 26:8 (NLT)**

Obedience has never been popular. It requires a humbling submission to some outside authority. It means you decide to do things that are not comfortable. It often entails considerable uncertainty about the outcome because obedience generally involves actions commanded by someone with a more complete grasp of the situation. And we who are called to that obedience must proceed with simple faith, but in the end . . . *"obedience is better than sacrifice"* (1 Samuel 15:22).

Such was the case with Navy Torpedo Squadron Eight (VT-8) at the battle of Midway in World War II. That battle occurred just six months after the Japanese attack on Pearl Harbor and its outcome would determine the entire course of the war. Historians regard this epic sea battle as the single most important naval battle of the Pacific Campaign of that war. If the Japanese could occupy Midway Island they could reach Hawaii with their bombers and position their surface ships to dominate most of the Pacific Ocean.

VT-8 was based aboard the aircraft carrier USS Hornet and equipped with obsolete TBD Devastator aircraft designed to deliver torpedoes from very low altitudes, normally about

Seven Stone Steps

200 feet. The planes were slow and ponderous and lacked any significant defensive armament. They were manned by one pilot and one gunner who were equipped with a single and entirely inadequate light machine gun.

When the Japanese fleet was located, 15 airplanes of VT-8, led by Lieutenant Commander John Waldron, launched from the USS Hornet with orders to attack at all cost. Those 30 men knew that this mission was critical, but that their airplanes were inadequate, that their tactics placed them in extreme danger, and that their chances of survival were limited. They also knew that they would receive no protection from their fighter planes because those had been assigned to protect the higher-flying dive bombers. Nevertheless, they simply obeyed their orders and proceeded towards the enemy fleet.

When the Japanese carriers were found, all fifteen VT-8 airplanes attacked, pressing their torpedo delivery to the closest possible range at altitudes that placed them in the greatest harm due to point blank anti-aircraft fire from the ships and swarms of enemy fighter planes. In a very short time, every one of VT-8's airplanes was destroyed and every crew member but one was killed. And no torpedoes hit the enemy. It would appear that their impressive obedience was a tragic mistake. Except...

Except, the courageous obedience of VT-8's aircrews actually achieved three results that were critical to the American victory at Midway. First, they kept the Japanese carrier force off balance so that they were unable to launch immediate counterattacks. Second, the low flying TBDs pulled the Japanese fighters out of their normal position at much higher altitude. Third, many of the enemy fighters ran low on ammunition and fuel during their attacks on the VT-8 airplanes.

Because of their obedience, the crews of VT-8 made it possible for the American dive bombers to attack the Japanese carriers unopposed. Those dive bombers, which arrived just after the torpedo attacks, encountered little opposition and were able to sink all four of the Japanese aircraft carriers, a blow from which the Japanese Navy never really recovered. Military historian John Keegan has described the victory at Midway as "the most stunning and decisive blow in the history of naval warfare."

And all agree that the single most important contribution to that pivotal victory was the selfless obedience of those 30 airmen of VT-8. *"Obedience is better than sacrifice."*

> "Obedience without faith is possible,
> but not faith without obedience."
> -Anonymous

> **Now that you know these things,
> you will be blessed if you do them.
> John 13:17**

Most people don't like the idea that their thoughts and their actions should be guided by an external force. They prefer to "be their own person" to "do it my way." They write songs about it. Personal freedom is an essential human condition.

Adam and Eve didn't like obedience. It limited their options.

Cain didn't like the concept so he killed his brother.

Abraham was an honorable man in a thousand ways but at two points he chose not to obey and thus put his own wife at peril.

Jacob lied, Jonah rebelled, Samson womanized, David murdered and Peter betrayed. Obedience is tough even for the big guys.

Seven Stone Steps

Some Christian theologians cringe at the mention of obedience because they fear the potential for legalism; they fear that people will think they can earn or maintain a relationship with God by obeying His laws. And, of course, that misunderstanding is always a risk, and any religion based on legalism would miss the mark. We are saved by grace—God's free and undeserved favor. But, we are saved by grace for a purpose: *"to do good works"* (Ephesians 2:10).

Others are rightly afraid that any mention of obedience will be distorted to mean obedience to some cultural norms. And those are good and righteous concerns since the church has a long history of inserting cultural behaviors as forms of required obedience: clothing styles, particular Bible versions, certain music, jewelry issues, gender-specific seating, etc.

But despite those concerns and objections we are called to obedience. Samuel confronted Saul with the blunt message that simple obedience was better than any sacrifice Saul could offer. Jesus said, *"If you love me, you will obey what I command"* (John 14:15). John included in his first letter, *"This is love for God: to obey his commands"* (1 John 5:3). The problem is that we are slow learners. Like Naaman (2 Kings 5).

Naaman was commander of the army of the king of Aram (Syria). Naaman was a powerful man with great authority and a fine reputation, but he was a man afflicted with leprosy. One of his wife's servants was a captured Israeli girl who apparently respected Naaman and pitied him for his affliction. This young girl recommended that Naaman go to Israel and seek the help of Elisha the prophet. And so he did. This powerful commander of thousands set out with his entire retinue of horses and chariots and servants to seek the advice of an obscure prophet of God. It was an impressive spectacle of wealth and power, and when Naaman arrived, the prophet gave him humbling and simple instructions for curing his disease: *"Wash yourself seven times in the Jordan River."*

Stepping Out in Obedience

Naaman had apparently expected some grand ceremony of ritual cleansing and prayers and incantations, but Elisha's instructions were so plain and simple that Naaman left angry. What possible good could be accomplished by bathing in this crude local river when he could have just stayed home and bathed in the much grander rivers of Syria? Why should he obey such a demeaning and pointless suggestion even if this man did claim to be an agent of God?

But Naaman's servants challenged him to consider that if he was willing to obey some grand and difficult command, why not obey this simple unpretentious one? Which he finally did. And that cured his leprosy immediately.

And so it is with us. We have those simple commands in Peter's second letter to *"goodness, knowledge, self-control, perseverance, godliness, brotherly kindness and love"* that we resist with human apathy and stubbornness even though as the modern martyr Jim Elliot said, "it is His business to lead, command, impel, send, call . . . and it is your business to obey, follow, move, respond . . . ."

And what if we did? What if we endeavored to obey those simple commands as Naaman obeyed Elisha? What cleansing would we experience?

> "Faith, as Paul saw it, was a living, flaming thing leading to surrender and obedience to the commandments of Christ."
> -A. W. Tozer

Through him and for his name's sake, we received grace and apostleship to call people . . . <u>to the obedience that comes from faith</u>.
Romans 1:5 (emphasis mine)

Seven Stone Steps

We are saved by grace, when we believe in faith, and for the purpose of doing good works. That is the God-given order of it. A personal, eternal relationship with Him on the basis of simple faith in His grace as demonstrated in the sacrificial death of Jesus, and then—and then obedience as a natural response of affection and gratitude for the work that has already been accomplished on the cross.

This is not the teeth-gritting sort of conformity that earns you points with your supervisor at work. It is the kind of obedience that is naturally given to a loving and caring Father. It is the obedience of a son or daughter who has boundless respect for his or her parent and who just genuinely wants to obey as a response of respect and esteem. Obedience is an agreeable and satisfying response of love for a merciful and gracious Father.

Gideon knew that (Judges 6). Gideon received some illogical and difficult instructions from God and responded with obedience because he loved the God of Israel.

Gideon was a farm boy. He had no military training and certainly no training in tactics and strategy. He was a farm boy, from the least of the tribes and the least family of that tribe. He was a simple farm boy comfortable with a scythe and a wine press but thoroughly uninformed in matters military. But Gideon was a lover and a follower of YAHWEH.

Gideon's first move was to destroy the idols and pagan altars that his family had erected. His first move was to make sure he was on certain, holy ground as he moved in obedience. Then he enlisted the aid of 32,000 men to attack the enemy, a number that was really inadequate for the task but what God had provided. Obedience is a matter of the heart, not a matter of resources.

But God told Gideon to send home anyone who *"trembled with fear,"* and so 22,000 men went home and Gideon's army was down to a pathetic ten thousand men. But, obedience is not dependent on numbers.

Apparently God thought the same thing because He then stripped Gideon's army down to 300 men, about what the Midianites would use to peel potatoes. Their army was so large that even the camels were beyond counting. And then with a mere 300 dedicated companions and the backing of the Sovereign God, Gideon utterly defeated the hordes of Midian and killed their generals.

Gideon's limitations are important to the story. God called him to lead an attack on the fearsome Midianites but without any personal resources or training to do so. If he had those resources and that training there would have been little room for faith in his obedience, robbing it of real meaning. It is the same with us. We are not always called to obedience in matters that are easy and painless. But we are always called to obedience in matters that are important to God, and it is faith that leads us to that personal surrender that results in obedience.

> "God is God. Because He is God, He is
> worthy of my trust and obedience.
> I will find rest nowhere but in His holy will,
> a will that is unspeakably beyond
> my largest notions of what He is up to."
> -Elisabeth Elliot

**His divine power has given us everything
we need for life and godliness through our
knowledge of him who called us
by his own glory and goodness.
Through these he has given us his very great and
precious promises, so that through them you may
participate in the divine nature and escape the
corruption in the world caused by evil desires.
2 Peter 1:3-4**

Seven Stone Steps

Peter begins his second letter with two verses of salutation and then a reminder of what has been done for the believer in Christ (verse 3), followed by a description of what the implications are (verse 4), and then some very specific instructions (verses 5-7) that require obedience. It is a heady statement of the great gifts that we have received from the very hand of God and the purpose for which those gifts were intended, with a call to obedience. And, it is the very topic of this book you are reading.

First, Peter says, we have been given everything we need and that by His divine glory and goodness, not by our diligent efforts. Blaise Pascal famously said that man has a "God-shaped hole in his heart." Peter is saying that God created the perfect filling for that "hole". Without God there is a missing element, a dark hole, a burning restlessness in the midst of a worldly corruption. But God has given everything we need for godly living, for eternity, to those who believe.

But there is more. He has given us great and precious promises. These promises are so great and so precious that they include the pledge that we—imagine this—*we* can participate in the very nature of God. We have been given the indwelling presence of God, His Holy Spirit, to empower us in all of this. Peter knew this well. He preached about it at Pentecost, and in that sermon he quoted the prophet Joel who foretold the Spirit's coming to men. Don't forget this. The indwelling Spirit is the reservoir of strength from which we are able to draw the power to develop the virtues that Peter describes.

Ezekiel promised *"I will put my Spirit in you so that you will follow my decrees and be careful to obey my regulations"* (Ezekiel 36:27, NLT, emphasis mine). It is a frequently missed dimension in any discussion of Christian living and obedience. Those who have been saved by grace through faith are temples of the Holy Spirit. When they strive for Godly virtue, they have that resource to propel them. It is somewhat like sailing a boat. I can maintain the boat in lovely condition. I can make all the right preparations; I can exercise great seamanship and boat handling. I can set the sails at exactly the right angle, but without the invisible wind to provide the power, I am becalmed.

So it is with our spiritual life. The Holy Spirit is the wind that empowers us in any effort to cultivate Godly virtue. In fact, the Greek word for Spirit (<u>pneuma</u>) can be and is also translated "wind." And thus, while we must pay due diligence to all of the basics while we cast off and raise the sails, we are helpless without the pneuma.

Peter says we have been given everything we need for Godly living, and that is an intimate relationship with the living God, the eternal hope of great and precious promises, and the means to escape the corruption that routinely drags us into thoughts and behavior that are destructive.

And the obvious question is, "What then?" Fortunately, Peter doesn't leave us hanging.

> "Obedience is the fruit of faith."
> -Christina Rossetti

For this very reason, make every effort to add to your faith goodness . . . knowledge . . . self-control . . . perseverance . . . godliness . . . brotherly kindness . . . and love.
2 Peter 1:5-7 (abbreviated)

Peter describes our foundation in verses three and four and then transitions to the statement *"for this very reason add to your faith."* He has given the reasons and now moves on to what we do about it. And what we do is *"add to our faith"* seven virtues that are really an outline of what it would be like to live out a life pleasing to God. In fact it is an outline of what it would be like to have the character of God.

Seven Stone Steps

"Add to your faith." Grace first. Faith first. Relationship first and then the appropriate response. It is important to get the sequence right because otherwise we miss the point of grace. Free grace. Undeserved grace. Grace with nothing earned or deserved, followed by a personal faith in that grace. And then *"add to your faith."*

The problem is that on one hand we long for some personal merit. We want to earn our relationship with God so we can feel good about ourselves. We want to do things and get the credit. Or, on the other hand, we are prone to abuse grace by expanding it to excuse our moral failures with clichés about "we're all sinners, aren't we?" and "God will love me anyway." Without some resolution of these two polar opposites the whole gospel is shackled. But Peter produces the key to those shackles.

"For this very reason" (because we have been adopted by the living God by grace through faith) *"for this very reason add to your faith"* the virtues that are pleasing to your adopted Father. With that synthesis Peter neatly joins grace and obedience. It is not "on the one hand and then the other"; it is two hands working in concert.

But what does he mean by *"add to your faith"*? What would that look like? For one thing it means we would carefully avoid what Moffat defines as nominal Christianity, "an initial spasm followed by chronic inertia."

From a positive view it means that we will strive to cultivate Godly virtues because they are pleasing to God and *"obedience is better than sacrifice."* Also, it would mean that we add those virtues for the stated reason: that we want to honor the one who loved us first, not because we need to earn His affections. And, in the end, we cannot avoid the fact that God, Abba, Father, Lord, is honored and pleased by the obedience that comes from faith.

And after that careful introduction, Peter commends to us seven virtues that are the appropriate ornaments for our faith: *goodness, knowledge, self-control, perseverance, godliness, brotherly kindness and love.* It is a call to step out in obedience and a call to step up in virtue.

> "A high calling followed by low living
> leads to deep suffering."
> -Sidlow Baxter

Do not merely listen to the word, and so deceive yourselves. Do what it says.
James 1:22

Joseph was obedient. And the results of his obedience were not apparent for a long time. But he was obedient and that was pleasing to God and effective for His purposes.

Joseph became a slave in Egypt where he was owned by a military official. He was an intelligent and reliable slave and so he was placed in charge of all the household affairs. That was as good as it got for a slave in Egypt.

But his owner's wife was a lustful, devious woman who sexually enticed young Joseph day by day. And each day this healthy, normal young man resisted her advances until she became so angry that she caused Joseph to be thrown in prison out of spite. Joseph's obedience must have appeared futile and worthless during that extended incarceration, but God had a plan. He always has a plan for our obedience.

In prison, Joseph met a man who had worked for the Pharaoh and through that connection Joseph's reputation as one who could interpret dreams brought him into the royal court where he eventually became second only to the Pharaoh in authority in Egypt and made it possible for the Jewish people to find refuge there.

Joseph's obedience had consequences far beyond Joseph's personal circumstances. His obedience eventually elevated him to a position of great power and authority and that position allowed Joseph to provide for his family during a crisis which allowed the Jewish nation to survive. The simple obedience of one man ultimately determined the fate of an entire race.

Obedience always has a purpose, although we seldom see it directly. *Goodness, knowledge, self-control, perseverance, godliness, brotherly kindness and love* all have eternal purposes even if we don't see them now. Nevertheless, we are called to obedience in those matters. It is all about stepping higher.

> "One act of obedience is better
> than one hundred sermons."
> -Dietrich Bonhoeffer

Wherefore, my beloved ones, as you always obeyed, not as in my presence only, but now much more in my absence, carry to its ultimate goal (likeness to the Lord Jesus Christ) your own salvation with a wholesome, serious caution and trembling, for God is the One who is supplying you the impulse, giving you both the power to resolve and the strength to perform His good pleasure.
Philippians 2:12-13, (Wuest Word Studies, Vol III)

Chapter Two

Stepping Higher in Virtue

"Sometimes it helps to know that I just can't
do it all. One step at a time is
all that's possible."
-Anne W. Schaef

**The path of life leads upward for the wise.
Proverbs 15:24**

There was a man who liked to spend his evenings in the local barroom, where he could avoid all the challenges of being a father and husband, and where alcohol numbed the anxieties of life. Then, after two or three hours of drinking and swapping lies, he would stumble home and fall in bed. His children were neglected, his finances ruined and his marriage was a train wreck.

One winter night as he walked to the same old bar through a few inches of new-fallen snow he sensed someone behind him. When he turned to look he saw his little son walking with exaggerated steps to match his tracks in the snow. When the dad asked his son, "What are you doing?" the boy replied, "I'm walking in your footsteps, dad."

It is what children do. They tend to walk in our footsteps for good or evil. As dads it is important where we walk, and as children of God, it is important for us to walk in our Savior's footsteps.

This book is about the cultivation of Christian virtues using Peter's instructions to the church in his second letter (2 Peter 1:3-5) that we *make every effort to add to your faith goodness, knowledge, self-control, perseverance, godliness, brotherly kindness, and love.*

Seven Stone Steps

It is not about earning your way to heaven or gaining merit points with God. It is about stepping up to Christian virtues because they represent the essence of God's character and because our goal is always to be more like Him. It is about pleasing a loving Father, not bargaining with a stern judge. It is about responding to a gift of love, not gaining favor with a demanding overseer. And this book is about trusting the indwelling Holy Spirit for daily encouragement to become more like the Savior, knowing in advance that we can never step that high but are nevertheless committed to stepping up one step at a time, always striving to step higher.

During my career as a pilot I spent many days in Paris. It is, as so many have said, a lovely city, and one of the sincere enjoyments of that city is to view it from the top platform of the Eiffel Tower. An elevator takes you straight up those 985 feet but there are also stairs—1665 steps from the street level to the top platform. Those steps are not enclosed and you can see clearly through the iron grid that surrounds them as you climb.

On one of those trips I had an unusual two day layover and so I decided that on the second full day I would make it a project to walk to the top of the tower. 1665 steps; 985 feet; about 100 stories. I knew it would be a long and taxing climb but I thought how it would be fun to climb without any schedule and see the city expand beneath me with each step higher. Even if it took all day, I would enjoy the challenge and the view.

That morning, I was ready with a small backpack with water and snacks and I started upwards in fine summer weather. The climb to the first level is something over 300 steps and it was all pleasant. That first level is a very large floor with multiple shops and food kiosks, so after a brief rest I started up to the second level. That was equally pleasant, although my legs were feeling the effects of climbing some 40 stories. I was enjoying the challenge and anticipating the final long climb to the top when

Stepping Higher in Virtue

I found that those stairs are closed to the public. It is almost 20 years later as I write this and I am still disappointed. I had planned and savored the climb from bottom to top and found that it was not possible. It cannot be climbed by tourists.

And so it is for those who would strive to climb higher in their Christian virtues. It is a good thing, a right thing and a rewarding and lovely thing which expands our view in every direction. It is a continuous process which never ends in this life but we are not capable of actually climbing to full Christ likeness. We can climb a long way but we cannot reach the top in this life. But, even knowing that, we climb.

> "God gave me hills to climb and
> strength for climbing."
> -Arthur Guiterman

Come, let us go up to the mountain of the LORD, to the house of the God of Jacob. He will teach us his ways, so that we may walk in his paths.
Isaiah 2:3

The concept inherent in this instruction by Peter to *add to your faith goodness, knowledge, self-control, perseverance, godliness, brotherly kindness, and love* is captured in a Greek word, askesis (as-kee-sis), that means to "strive" or "contend" with the dedication of an athlete. It is the grit and determination to finish the race and finish well.

Peter is not talking about harsh fasts or severe personal denial. He is not describing in this passage some Eastern form of austerity but a commitment to personal striving after spiritual maturity through simple virtues. Paul instructed his young friend Timothy to *"train yourself to be godly"* (1 Timothy 4:7). The verb we translate as "train" is the Greek word (gumnazo) from which we derive our English word gymnasium.

Seven Stone Steps

So, just as an athlete disciplines his body at the gym, we can exercise similar disciplines in our spiritual life. And just as the athlete depends on his trainer for encouragement and direction, so we can depend on the Holy Spirit. The athlete's goal is physical strength. Peter's direction here is for us to develop spiritual and personal strength for a world that powerfully draws us toward selfish, apathetic and impatient behavior. Paul encourages every Christian to become a spiritual athlete, and Peter describes some worthy targets for our fitness program: *goodness, knowledge, self control, perseverance, godliness, brotherly kindness and love.* And, as we will see, these virtues build on each other from the simple foundation of *goodness* to the final excellence of *love.* It is a spiritual exercise in climbing higher.

All of this is based on the simple precept that when we are stressed, physically or spiritually, we do not rise to the occasion; we fall to our level of preparation. Navy Seals, Air Force fighter pilots and Army snipers do not rise to the demands of combat because they have been given a job description and a badge. Christians do not rise to the occasion because they have been adopted by their Father. All of the above can only perform at the level to which they have submitted to discipline and training. *"And for this very cause, having added on your part every intense effort, provide lavishly in your faith . . ."* (1 Peter 1:5, Wuest translation, emphasis mine).

> "There is a great market for religious experience in our world; there is little enthusiasm for the patient acquisition of virtue, little inclination to sign up for the long apprenticeship in what earlier generations of Christians called holiness."
> -Eugene Peterson

> **He has showed you, O man, what is good.**
> **And what does the LORD require of you?**
> **To act justly and to love mercy**
> **and to walk humbly with your God.**
> **Joel 6:8**

There is cause for confusion over this issue of developing virtues because human nature naturally longs for some legal system of behavior that defines our goodness and rewards our efforts. We want a report card with high marks and we want to show it to our Father as a means of gaining His favor while advancing our self-esteem and our reputation.

God's economy doesn't work like that. The central issue is relationship—a relationship between a Father and His adopted child. It is about love as the foundation, and then working out of that relationship that is fixed, permanent and eternal. Father and child, loving one another—and since it started with Him, it is about how we can effectively and appropriately love Him in return. *"We love him, because he first loved us"* (1 John 4:19, KJV).

We have adopted children in our family. In the United States (and most countries) it is an interesting legal event. When a child is adopted even her birth certificate is issued anew with the adoptive parents' names and birth data. The adopted child is entitled to all the rights and privileges of a blood descendant and is subject to the complete legal authority of the parents. It is a solemn and binding commitment on both sides. And such are we who have connected with God's grace through personal faith: *"How great is the love the Father has lavished on us, that we should be called children of God! And that is what we are"* (1 John 3:1).

When the apostle Paul wrote about our adoption he had a Roman perspective, and the Roman concept of adoption was well fixed in law and practice. The adopted child became in every respect the legal child and heir of the adopting father. If the adopting father was a member of the patrician class, the new child inherited all of those rights and privileges regardless of his background. The best known case is that of the Roman emperor Augustus whose original name was Octavian. Augustus (see Luke 2:1) was arguably the most powerful and successful of all Roman emperors but mark this. . . Octavian/Augustus would have lived out the drab life of an ordinary Roman if he had not been adopted by Julius Caesar. That legal transaction placed Augustus in the line of imperial succession and everything changed after that.

And such are we who have become Christ followers: adopted sons and daughters with all the privileges and responsibilities that implies. But, then what?

> "These are commands but more on the
> order of invitations by the King.
> And, who can refuse the King?"
> -Anonymous

**For those God foreknew he also predestined to be conformed to the likeness of his Son, that he might be the firstborn among many brothers.
Romans 8:29**

Who can refuse a king indeed? Or a Father? Or a Father King?

God issued Ten Commandments as a means of expressing His holy nature but also to convince us that we are flawed creatures without the courage or the moral fiber to fully, completely keep those laws. They are God's perfect standard, and while we make feeble attempts and succeed in small parts, the entire collection is too much. We simply don't measure up to His canon of perfection. *"For whoever keeps the whole law and yet stumbles at just one point is guilty of breaking all of it"* (James 2:10).

But there is more. In addition to the Ten Commandments, this Father has ordained several lists of virtues that are declared for the Christ follower. You can find such lists in Colossians, Galatians, Ephesians, Romans, 1 Corinthians, 1 Timothy, Proverbs and elsewhere. The lists are there. They are an integral part of Scripture. They are there for a purpose—as is all of Scripture—and we would be remiss to pass over them as some type of technical regulations, imagining that God is not interested in genuine virtue. He is. He said so. He gave us the lists. He is calling us to climb higher because higher brings us closer to Him.

But, who can refuse a king? Or a Father? These lists are included in Scripture because they capture for us the very nature of God in practical elements. When we are told to *"clothe ourselves in compassion, kindness, humility, gentleness and patience"* (Colossians 3:12), it is not an edict on which our relationship with God depends but an insight into the virtues that define the Father and which He longs to see in us. Who can refuse a Father?

When we are told that love is defined as *patient, kind, not envious, boastful or proud; protecting, trustful, hopeful, etc* (1 Corinthians 13:4-7), it is not to intimidate us with a rulebook of suitable behavior, but to define for us the kind of love that is pleasing to God. And who can refuse a Father?

Lists can be intimidating or helpful. I like all of these lists because they help me to understand just what it looks like to be an adopted son of the King. I don't have to walk in the dark. I don't have to imagine. I have actual and practical steps. These are clear descriptions of my goal in all of this, but they are not lists of requirements for continued relationship. I am adopted, after all. The legal process has been completed. The new birth certificate has been issued. I am a legal and binding son, by grace through faith. Nothing can change that. If you are uncertain, read Romans 8:31-39.

So we come full circle. There are multiple lists of virtues that God has purposely included in His divine revelation. They are part of God's inspired word. These lists that are scattered throughout the Bible are clearly lists of behaviors pleasing to the Father. In recent years there has been much discussion of "love languages" for spouses—how to best express our affection and commitment to our married partners. In a similar way the biblical lists of virtues are best seen as God's love languages. They are the virtues that please Him and honor Him and delight Him. These are what He loves in His children.

And, who can refuse a Father?

> "The heights charm us, but the steps do not;
> with the mountain in our view
> we love to walk the plains."
> -Johann Wolfgang Von Goethe

> **I lift up my eyes to the hills—**
> **where does my help come from?**
> **My help comes from the LORD,**
> **the Maker of heaven and earth.**
> **Psalm 121:1-2**

During my college summers I worked for a painting contractor in Somerville, MA. Most of the buildings we painted were three-level, three-family units. They were old, wood frame buildings, mostly neglected, with their tricolor paint schemes faded and chipped. I was the youngest and sometimes the only sober member of that paint crew and so I always drew the assignment to paint the peaks in front.

Stepping Higher in Virtue

The longest ladder available was a 40-foot extension that reached only to a point about eight feet below the peak when fully extended. The houses were very close to the street so the ladder had to be rigged from the asphalt, which was potentially slippery, and it was also an obstruction for passing cars. Just climbing the fully extended ladder was a challenge with three paint pots and brushes and other tools, but when I got to the top there was a final test.

Normally it is impossible to work any higher than the third highest rung of an extension ladder. Even that step is somewhat precarious, but it can be done with care. The second and last steps are simply impossible to work from because of balance issues, except . . . On these houses I had to work not from the second rung or the first, but actually from the very top of the stringers—the very tip-top of the ladder sides. Here is how it can be done, but don't try this at home.

First you climb to the third highest step with a very large screw-hook, a hammer and a large screw driver. Standing on that third step you lean flat against the building and reach over your head as high as possible to blindly tap the screw-hook into the building with the hammer hoping to connect with some structural member under the siding. When the hook is fairly seated you reach up with the screw driver—still blind because you can't look up and stay balanced against the building—and use that screw driver as a lever to twist the hook as deeply as possibly.

When the hook is firmly seated you carefully hang the tools on your work belt and grab the hook above you, gently. Then try some weight on it, and then some more, until you are satisfied that it will support your full weight. Finally, when you are confident that the hook is set well enough, use it as your handhold to climb to the very tip of the uprights with paint and brush to reach the very top of the peak. It is a scary, dangerous procedure but it is also exhilarating to be up there and it is satisfying to see the completed work. There is something fundamentally exciting about climbing high even when there is risk involved. And that exposes an interesting contrast in human nature.

First, we all enjoy heights. Even those who say they are afraid are normally enthralled by the experience of seeing the world from a great elevation. Some enjoy the view of wilderness from the top of a hill or mountain. Many love the experience of seeing a great metropolitan area from the top of a building or tower: the Empire State Building in New York or the Eiffel Tower in Paris or the AMP Tower in Sidney. Others love the outlook from an airplane window as the landscape spreads out several miles below them. There are few people who do not enjoy the excitement of climbing higher in some form and surveying the world from that perspective.

Except—except there seems to be some indwelt inertia about climbing higher in our spiritual lives. We lift our eyes up to God's hills and we have a desire to climb but "with the mountains in view we love to walk the plains." Despite our best intentions, there is an essential human indifference about developing the virtues involved in stepping up from apathetic, ordinary faith to the behavior that was designed by God for us to express our love for Him. Let me go to church and read my daily devotional tweet but don't expect me to take the personal and social risks involved in adding virtue to my faith. The steps are too big. Climbing is hard. The reward may not be worth the effort. I may fall. Inertia is real. "The heights charm us but the steps do not."

The seven virtues that Peter decrees in his second letter are intended to define behaviors that are appropriate for a Christ follower. They lead us up. They are God's love language. They do not change the fundamental relationship but they invite us to climb up to a closer fellowship.

Stepping Higher in Virtue

There is nothing easy about becoming good, knowledgeable (about Godly issues), self-controlled, persevering, Godly, kindly and loving. Developing those virtues demands commitment and desire and a steady dependence on the indwelling Spirit of God, but up is good. Up is pleasing to the Father; it is what He loves and that is why we want to begin. Sometimes it is scary and sometimes demanding; sometimes it requires stretching and reaching in ways that others may think unusual or even hazardous, but then, who can refuse a Father?

Four young boys were plotting some mischief. As they considered the deed itself and the possible consequences they each mentioned their worst fears . . .

"My Dad will blow up if he hears about this."
"My Dad will beat the tar out of me if he finds out."
"My Dad will ground me for a month."
And the fourth thought quietly for a moment and said, "My Dad's heart will be broken if he hears that I did this."

What a good and right reason to develop God-ordained virtues. "My Father's heart will be broken if I don't even try."

> "I do not at all understand the mystery of grace—only that it meets us where we are but does not leave us where it found us."
> -Anne Lamott

For it is by grace you have been saved, through faith—and this not from yourselves, it is the gift of God—not by works, so that no one can boast. For we are God's workmanship, created in Christ Jesus to do good works, which God prepared in advance for us to do.
Ephesians 2:8-10

Seven Stone Steps

We sing enthusiastically of "Amazing Grace . . . that taught my heart to fear . . . then relieved those fears . . . and saved a wretch like me; grace that brought me safe thus far . . . and the grace that will lead me home." It is all true. It is all by grace, all by unmerited and unwarranted Divine favor. Amazing grace. Astounding. Astonishing. Amazing.

And out of that grace and mercy there is only one great response—love, for the One who is the author of mercy and the Giver of grace. Love for the Abba Father who has adopted us; love for the Son who died for us and intercedes for us; love for the Holy Spirit who instructs us and comforts us. It is all about the love of God and our love for God. If that is right, truly right, the rest will all follow naturally.

But, like the little drummer boy, what can I give Him? Maybe there is something. Maybe these virtues He has proclaimed are just the thing. If He has prescribed specific virtues for us wouldn't it be appropriate to respond with some diligent effort in that direction? When fathers explain desired conduct to their children, are they not pleased to see positive results? Is my Abba Father any different in that respect? Wouldn't His heart rejoice if I made *"every effort to add to my faith <u>goodness</u>; and to goodness, <u>knowledge</u>; and to knowledge, <u>self-control</u>; and to self-control, <u>perseverance</u>; and to perseverance, <u>godliness</u>; and to godliness, <u>brotherly kindness</u>; and to brotherly kindness, <u>love</u>"* (2 Peter 1:5-7, emphasis mine)?

This book is about the cultivation of Christian virtues. It is about climbing higher, closer to God by learning His love languages and cultivating them, nourishing them, and nurturing them through the power of the Holy Spirit that makes our body God's temple.

Stepping Higher in Virtue

"Let me never undervalue or neglect any part of Thy revealed will. May I duly regard the doctrine and the practice of the Gospel, prizing its commands as well as its promises."
-Anonymous Puritan prayer

**It is God who arms me with strength and makes my way perfect. He makes my feet like the feet of a deer; he enables me to stand on the heights.
Psalm 18:32**

Chapter Three

The Step of Goodness

"So good a thing is virtue (goodness) that
even its enemies applaud and admire it."
-St. John Chrysostom

**For this very reason, make every effort
to add to your faith goodness . . .
2 Peter 1:5**

You heard it often from your mother, "Be good." It was an ambiguous instruction to exhibit a general demeanor of kindness, integrity and decency as you went through the activities of the day. "Be good." The problem was, while you had some vague notion of what that meant, it was, well, vague. And, what your mother meant might not be entirely the same thing that Peter means when he directs us to add "goodness" to our faith.

In fact, the idea expressed by the word translated "goodness" *is* challenging to capture in English. Bible translators have used "moral excellence," "virtue," and "worthiness" to express the original meaning in English but they are all somewhat inadequate. The Greek word used here is <u>aretay</u> (ar-et-ay), a word that has the general meaning of virtue, but virtue with a Greek cultural slant.

Greek culture placed a high value on strength, courage, perseverance, etc. Aretay was the robust goodness or worthiness associated with masculine moral excellence. Modern critics might criticize that emphasis as sexist but a more positive view (a more correct view) would be to describe it as a striving to emphasize those masculine attributes that are critical to a safe and secure society. There is no reason to think that aretay was meant to diminish the feminine gender. It was more probably meant to elevate those male qualities that are vital to the stability of any civilization, including the moral and physical protection of women. Men and women are different. We need each other. We need the strength and physical gallantry of men for production and protection, and we need the intuitive, gentler nature of women for stability, all in combination, for any serious culture to thrive.

The root meaning of the Greek aretay is manliness as understood by the Greeks. It is the kind of manliness that we associate with chivalry: courtesy, generosity, compassion and kindness, with great strength and courage. It is the kind of manliness that combines vigor with humility and the best of what could and should be of men. Aretay. "Goodness" works just fine when you understand the basis. *"Add to your faith goodness."*

"Virtue is bold and goodness never fearful."
-Shakespeare

His divine power has given us everything
we need for life and godliness through our
knowledge of him who called us
by his own glory and goodness.
2 Peter 1:3

And this goodness prescribed for us is the very goodness that God Himself demonstrates. Regardless of the words used by the translators of your personal Bible, the original Greek word is the same for Peter's description of God's goodness (verse 3) and the goodness we are called to add to our faith (verse 5). "He called us by His own glory and aretay" and He calls us to "add aretay to our faith."

Further, Shakespeare describes the root meaning of this goodness very well; it is bold and it is not fearful. This kind of goodness is assertive and active. It is different from your Mom's goodness because it is much more than that passive goodness that simply refrains from evil. Your Mom wanted you to stay out of trouble. Peter is advocating a goodness that is much stronger than that. He is saying that we should move into an active practice of good, or virtue, or moral excellence. Take your pick. Peter has begun his list with a word that captures the sum of all desirable character qualities. It is a broad, inclusive term, but with the overtones of masculine strength coupled with genuine humility.

In the 1970s, William Crawford was a janitor in one of the dormitories at the U.S. Air Force Academy. His work there was simple, menial labor: mopping floors, cleaning toilets and generally keeping the spaces tidy. It was humble work accomplished faithfully by an unassuming man who was much more than just unassuming.

"Bill" was described by the young students there as a quiet, plain man who worked in the background and had little to say other than "Hello." He was older and slower and quieter than the ambitious cadets. He was shy and essentially invisible in the supercharged world of an elite military academy. He just did his job well without drawing attention to himself.

At some point, one of the young cadets was reading a history of the intense ground campaign in Italy during World War II. One part of that book related the story of a Private William Crawford who was assigned to the 36th Infantry Division and who had been involved in some extreme and bloody infantry combat near the town of Altavilla. The story continued, "in the face of intense and hostile fire, with no regard for personal safety, and on his own initiative, Private Crawford single-handedly attacked fortified enemy positions." But there was more.

Seven Stone Steps

After the battle, Bill Crawford was captured by the Germans and presumed dead. His heroism that day was so exceptional that he was awarded the Medal of Honor which, in his absence, was presented to his dad. The citation included the solemn words used to describe the heroic virtue of every recipient of that most distinguished of all military honors in the United States: "For Conspicuous Gallantry and Intrepidity in Action at the Risk of Life, Above and Beyond the Call of Duty." The Medal of Honor is the highest military decoration awarded by any branch of the military. It is an honor that was awarded to only 464 men out of the more than six million who served during World War II.

The historical record reported that later in the year of 1945 Bill Crawford was rescued from German captivity and went on to retire from the Army as a Master Sergeant after 23 years of honorable service. Bill Crawford was a living example of goodness in his selfless service, his bravery and his humility. He was positively and assertively good and he was quietly and gently humble. *"Add to your faith goodness."*

Incidentally, when Bill Crawford—this humble janitor—died in 1980, the Governor of Colorado declared that all of that state's flags be lowered to half staff in his honor.

> "Mediocrity is never God's will for us. He calls us to excellence and challenges us to be more than we thought."
> -Max Browning

If anything is excellent (aretay)
—think about such things.
Philippians 4:8 (explanation mine)

Add to your faith goodness even if it seems unobserved and unappreciated like Bill Crawford's janitorial work at the Air Force Academy.

The Step of Goodness

In the summer of 1967, I was unemployed for seven weeks while my airline was shut down due to a strike by the mechanic's union. My wife had just given birth to our third child and we did not have an emergency fund, so I immediately looked for temporary work and found a job flying a small helicopter over Manhattan and Coney Island and Yankee Stadium with an electric sign advertising a soft drink, "Yoo Hoo Mountain Dew." I had flown helicopters in the Navy and enjoyed returning to those very different aircraft for a short time, especially during the lovely summer months.

One of the most engaging sights of the New York City area is the Statue of Liberty. From the clear bubble of that little helicopter, flying at low level, I could see the excellent detail of the Lady's hair and shoulders and the torch on the very top of the statue. It is interesting to note the fine workmanship even on the very top of the statue, an area that the sculptor could not have expected anyone to see, ever. Remember that the statue was made in the early 1880s and the first practical helicopters were not built until the 1940s. Nevertheless, the very top of that great colossus is as finely wrought as the most visible portions below. It is an image of the goodness/excellence that Peter advocates for our moral behavior. Add to your faith goodness even if it seems unobserved and unappreciated.

> "No man or woman can be strong, gentle,
> pure, and good, without the world being
> better for it and without someone being
> helped and comforted by the
> very existence of that goodness."
> -Phillips Brookes

Do good to them that hate you.
Matthew 5:44

Seven Stone Steps

One of the great stories of goodness—strong, assertive goodness—is contained in a few short verses in the very last chapter of the book of Genesis. It is a climax to the sweeping story of Joseph, the patriarch, which occupies more than one-quarter of the entire book of Genesis.

As a teen, Joseph had suffered a death threat by his jealous older brothers, but then, after being robbed by them and imprisoned in a cistern, they sold him into slavery. It was sibling rivalry before the term was invented. His own brothers had stolen from him, abused him, sold him to foreigners as a slave, and then lied about it all to their father. Joseph was dragged in chains to Egypt and sold to a wealthy man as household help.

There is much more to this amazing story in which Joseph survives years in prison and eventually rises to a position which is superseded only by the Pharaoh himself. In the end those very same brothers come begging for food in the midst of a famine and find their exploited brother has risen to such prominence and authority that he has the very power of life and death over them. Considering their former behavior, these brothers have every reason to believe they will be imprisoned or executed or both. But they are surprised by Joseph, who not only spares their lives but promises protection and support for them and their families. Joseph saw the scope of his life and misfortunes through the eyes of his God and could recognize that while his brothers *intended to harm him, God intended it for good to accomplish the saving of many lives (Genesis 50:20).*

Joseph's action was far more than your Mom's "Be good." Joseph exercised a manly, proactive goodness that carried the risk of exposing him as a political weakling and offending the Pharaoh but with the potential benefit of saving not only his brothers but the entire future of the Jewish race. Joseph's decision was *aretay* before there ever was a Greek language.

The Step of Goodness

> "Of all virtues and dignities of the mind,
> goodness is the greatest, being the
> character of the Deity; and without it, man is
> a busy, mischievous, wretched thing."
> -Francis Bacon

**Prove all things; hold fast that which is good.
1 Thessalonians 5:21**

In the end it helps to remember that the aretay that Peter commends is the same aretay that God has demonstrated from the beginning. It is a goodness that proceeds without fear of criticism or rebuke. It is goodness that does not measure the cost. It is goodness that is decisive and persevering and focused on others, and in the end it often appears strange, weird, and bizarre.

It also helps to consider that this goodness is not a quality that is natural to human nature. Feodor Dostoevsky (1821-1881) was one of Russia's greatest authors. His writing explores the workings of human psychology and spirituality in the context of Russia during the turbulent years of that century and he does so in a way that transcends time and place. His understanding of the human character was profound, but his ability to translate that into riveting prose was genius.

One of his great works was the novel, "The Idiot." The title comes from the central character, a man named Myshkin, who, although he suffered from epilepsy, was considered to be an idiot primarily for other reasons. In the novel, Myshkin strives to live out the Christian life and all of its virtues. He is compassionate, patient, humble, forgiving and otherwise "good"—aretay good. In fact Myshkin's goodness is so contrary to the behavior of other people that those around him consider him to be naïve and simple-minded. They assume that he has no understanding of the very real difficulties and dilemmas of normal life. In modern terms they don't think that he "gets it." They think he is an idiot.

And so did some of those around Jesus.

And so, undoubtedly, will others when we act out this aretay goodness in a thoughtless and selfish world. I have wonderful friends who have adopted 14 children to add to their family of four natural children. They have spent their lives and limited fortunes on this extreme family and while many admire them there are those who consider them curious or even eccentric.

Goodness is simply not a quality that is natural to human nature. Neither is it some passive niceness. Aretay goodness is the robust kind that acts outside the box; a goodness that thinks more of my companions than myself in the midst of combat; a goodness that adopts 14 children and commits life to providing the loving, orderly structure of a Godly household. It risks criticism for violating rigid customs and it risks life itself to protect friends in harm.

Certainly we are capable of good things and people around us demonstrate that frequently, but that goodness is like a spark which needs nurturing to create a larger fire. When Peter instructs us to add goodness to our faith he is encouraging us to do so in a dynamic and robust way that will entail risks and inconvenience and sacrifice.

Because this goodness stuff is somewhat vague and imprecise, it can be helpful to remove some of the clutter from our thinking about what it might mean. It can help to expunge some "goodness" concepts that can be misleading.

- This goodness that Peter encourages is not the passive kind of goodness that simply avoids conflict.
- It is not an introverted goodness that merely shuns evil.

The Step of Goodness

- It is not a private goodness that withdraws from the ugly realities of life.
- It is not simple good manners and courtesy, although those may play a small part.
- It is not reactive good behavior but proactive, robust goodness that may, at times, defy customs, confront tradition and offend beliefs. It may, in fact, appear to be idiotic.

Aretay is a hearty goodness that seeks to overcome the evil in the world in all its forms: indifference, apathy, dishonesty, arrogance, cruelty, bigotry, violence, and . . . well, assemble your own list. There is no lack of inequity in the world and when we *add goodness to our faith* it is a commitment to overcome those with the opposite and conflicting behavior, which can lead to personal risk and discomfort but is nevertheless the very thing intended.

"For this very reason, add to your faith goodness . . ."

When it is done right, there are few things more valuable, more noble or more satisfying. Ask Bill Crawford. Ask Joseph. Ask the parents who have adopted troubled children. Ask your Mom.

> "It is easy to perform a good action,
> but not easy to acquire a settled habit
> of performing such actions."
> -Aristotle

**For you, O LORD, have delivered
my soul from death
my eyes from tears
my feet from stumbling
that I may walk before the LORD
in the land of the living.
Psalm 116:8-9**

Chapter Four

The Step of Knowledge

*"Of all the kinds of knowledge that we can
obtain, the knowledge of God
and the knowledge of ourselves
are the most important."
-Jonathan Edwards*

**But grow in the grace and knowledge of our
Lord and Savior Jesus Christ. To him be glory
both now and forever! Amen.
2 Peter 3:18**

Peter begins his list of recommended virtues with that generalized encouragement to "goodness," but a robust kind of goodness that has the strength and endurance to set the foundation for others to follow. He then follows up with an encouragement to "knowledge." *"For this very reason, add to your faith . . . knowledge."*

So the immediate question is, "What kind of knowledge?" Peter is clearly not interested here in your understanding of particle physics or constitutional law. He is talking about the kind of knowledge that is consistent with his initial encouragement to goodness. He is encouraging us to spiritual knowledge that is in accord with everything else he and the other authors of Scripture have written. It is knowledge of God and God's priorities and purposes and how we fit into that great plan. *"For this very reason, add to your faith . . . knowledge."*

Think of our human situation like this: We are all like people who have been born in a room without windows. We can move about in that room and form relationships with others in that room, and those relationships generate theories about truth and reality that are simply theories because we need a window to see outside the room in order to grasp ultimate reality. Without that window we simply speculate and philosophize and theorize endlessly about what is, what could be and what should be just as two casual friends drinking coffee. Theories rise and fall in popularity but a clear view of truth is unavailable in that room. It is a room filled with speculation but without access to truth. It is certainly possible to live a long and healthy life in that room, but it would be a life without knowledge of reality. For that knowledge we must be able to see beyond the walls of that room and come to know the bigger truth, the real truth. We need a window to see.

God has given us the Bible as that window to reality outside the box, and His Word is the source of the knowledge that Peter exhorts us toward in this passage. *"Add to your faith . . . knowledge."* Look through the window. Ignore the incessant theological theories generated inside the box.

Now, consider a man who finally sets out to purchase a Bible because he has been told it is a window to reality. He carefully inspects the many various translations and editions to find the one that best suits him. He chooses an attractive, leather cover and even has his name inscribed in gold letters and then he takes his new possession home. His challenge from that point will be to recognize that he has purchased a window but he needs to open it and look deeply at what is outside his life-box. He has not purchased the wisdom and knowledge contained in those many pages, he has only bought the pages themselves. If the Bible becomes a table ornament in his living room he has wasted his money. If he makes a diligent effort to gaze out that window, to search and understand the content, he will slowly but surely see and recognize the knowledge that can transform his life and that of others. At first he will be like the blind man healed by Jesus in the eighth chapter of Mark, he will see but without great clarity, *"I see people; they look like trees walking around."* But also, like this same man, he will eventually see more clearly, *"Then his eyes were opened, his sight was restored, and he saw everything clearly"* (Mark 8:24, 25).

That is the knowledge that Peter refers to. It is the knowledge of God and the knowledge of ourselves and how those two have been brilliantly exposed in the 66 window panes that we call books of this revelation given directly from God to man. *"For this very reason, add to your faith . . . knowledge."*

> "The doorstep to the temple of wisdom
> is the knowledge of our own ignorance."
> -Charles Haddon Spurgeon

**The fear of the LORD is the beginning
of knowledge, but fools despise
wisdom and discipline.
Proverbs 1:7**

The Greek word <u>gnosis</u> (no-sis) that Peter uses here is the common Greek word for knowing or knowledge and, especially in the New Testament, spiritual knowledge. It is a word used 28 times in the New Testament. It is used by Jesus, when He chastised the spiritual leadership of Israel for "taking away the key to knowledge" (Luke 11:52); by Paul, when he reminds us that knowledge alone leads to pride and must be tempered with love (1 Corinthians 8:1), by Peter who encourages us to grow in our knowledge of Christ (2 Peter 3:18). It is a simple Greek word that any school child of that time would understand, but in Peter's command—and in most of the New Testament references—it is the word that means a knowledge of the things of God and how they apply to our thinking, our family, our work, our service, our faith, our life and death. It is the gnosis of God's will for us. It is knowledge with feet and hands. *"Add to your faith . . . knowledge."*

Seven Stone Steps

The Pharisees had abundant knowledge. They understood all of the sacred Scriptures and the Jewish cultural law, but they lacked the wisdom or judgment to apply that knowledge appropriately. Some professional teachers and professors have acquired a lifetime of knowledge without ever making that knowledge a useful and valuable part of their lives and influence.

I remember as a young man in my 30's hearing the Gospel of Christ, buying a Bible, reading it often, and listening to broadcast sermons. There was a lot of knowledge to be processed but I was a skeptic and a slow learner. At some point I understood the facts of grace and forgiveness and salvation sufficiently to teach a class on the essential issues. I had knowledge but nothing more. Certainly, that knowledge was an essential ingredient, but I needed that gnosis—that window outside of my box—in order to challenge my preconceptions about life and eternity which had been shaped in the context of a liberal university, hostile to the Gospel and committed to a secular worldview. I needed something more to make that knowledge effective.

I was at the doorstep of wisdom by virtue of knowing my own ignorance and the basic theology of grace, but at that point I had no faith to which I could add the knowledge. Eventually that faith came as a gift from God and the knowledge I had accumulated became real and meaningful and coherent. *"For this very reason, add to your faith . . . knowledge."*

> "To be conscious that you are ignorant
> is a great step to knowledge."
> -Benjamin Disraeli

**His divine power has given us everything
we need for life and godliness through our
knowledge of him who called us
by his own glory and goodness.
2 Peter 1:3**

So, all of these virtues are grounded and rooted in a personal faith. *"Add to your faith."* That robust goodness the Greeks called aretay and which begins Peter's list of seven virtues only works when it is embedded in faith—faith that God is, faith that God cares, faith that God is good, wise and sovereign, faith that we individuals are sinners in need of a Savior.

Similarly, the knowledge gnosis that Peter mentions second in this list of virtues is, in fact, an abiding, growing knowledge of Christ, *"who called us by His glory and goodness."* (verse 3); and it is a knowledge that promises to make you effective and productive in Christian living (verse 8). A promise—God's promise.

Nor should it be surprising that there are multiple dimensions of this knowledge. It is a layered knowledge which reaches both horizontally to our human relationships and vertically to our personal relationship with a loving, caring God.

On a personal basis this knowledge begins vertically with an understanding of God's forgiveness. It is the first thing we see through that window—God's gracious offer of forgiveness.

This concept is uniquely Christian and biblical. It is the knowledge that our relationship with God is not predicated on family or behavior or custom or liturgy. It is knowing that our relationship with God is based solely and completely on His grace revealed through the sacrifice of His Son and available freely to all who believe. It is not dependent on your past behavior because nothing is unforgiveable for those who seek forgiveness purely and solely on the finished work of The Lamb of God. *"It is finished."*

The final and ultimate sacrifice has been made and it has been made for anyone who believes. In this sense, it is more than just knowledge of Christ but acknowledgment that he is our only hope.

But there is much more. There is much knowledge that can be added to our faith and each element of that knowledge draws us deeper and closer to the one true God. What follows are a few particular elements of that knowledge and each one is broad and deep enough to satisfy a lifetime of learning and curiosity. *"Add to your faith . . . knowledge."*

> "Wisdom is the right use of knowledge. To know is not to be wise. Many men know a great deal, and are all the greater fools for it. There is no fool so great a fool as a knowing fool. But to know how to use knowledge is to have wisdom."
> -Charles Haddon Spurgeon

And this I pray, that your love may abound yet more and more in knowledge and in all judgment.
Philippians 1:9

So there is a practical purpose for this knowledge that Peter decrees. It is knowledge intended to produce wisdom in thought and actions in order to make us effective and productive (see verse 8). And it is knowledge that can be partitioned into specific topics. Consider . . .

It is the knowledge of God's majesty and greatness. Infinite power and wisdom and omniscience. King of all Kings for eternity, but also good and wise and loving. For the Christ-follower, it is knowing that the very same God who holds everything in the palm of His hand has also adopted us into His family as children who can approach Him as any King's children would do, with honor and respect and awe but with confidence in His affections and tender care. It is knowing that *"nothing is impossible with God"* (Luke 1:37), that *"great is our Lord and mighty in power; his understanding has no limit"* (Psalm 147:5), and that *"you did not receive a spirit that makes you a slave again to fear, but you received the Spirit of sonship. And by him we cry, 'Abba, Father'"* (Romans 8:15).

It is knowledge of the sickness of our own heart. It is the clear recognition that our instinctive motives are selfish and secular. If you doubt that, consider the front page of any newspaper or the struggles of your family or the routine contentions in the workplace. It is a foundational biblical truth that we are not naturally good and nice. Certainly we are capable of great and generous things, but those occur only when our natural bent is overcome. It is knowing that *"the hearts of men, moreover, are full of evil and there is madness in their hearts while they live"* (Ecclesiastes 9:3), that *"the heart is deceitful above all things and beyond cure"* (Jeremiah 17:9), and that *"from within, out of men's hearts, come evil thoughts, sexual immorality, theft, murder, adultery, greed, malice, deceit, lewdness, envy, slander, arrogance and folly. All these evils come from inside and make a man 'unclean'"* (Mark 7:21-23).

It is knowledge of God's offer of forgiveness for our sins and His charge that we forgive others in a similar fashion. It is knowing this link between our depravity and God's mercy and the logic that those who have been forgiven should (and must) freely forgive those who offend them.

That knowledge was wonderfully demonstrated by the South African government under the presidency of Nelson Mandela. President Mandela, a black man, assumed the presidency of that country after more than a century of vile and violent suppression of the blacks by the white majority.

When Nelson Mandela, himself one of the oppressed blacks, was elected president after 27 years in prison he could have begun a program of revenge against the white oppressors as was done in several other African nations. Many others urged him to do so.

Seven Stone Steps

Instead President Mandela, who had personally suffered a lifetime of persecution by the white majority, instituted the "Truth and Reconciliation Commissions" to bring a state of accord between blacks and whites after years of abuse, cruelty, and fighting, in order to prevent the natural vengeance and retaliation that was sure to occur with a newly elected black government.

It worked like this: Anyone who had perpetrated violence of any kind, even murder or rape or kidnapping could come to a commission, confess their crimes publicly, and receive amnesty from both civil and criminal prosecution. It was a rare, incredible, wonderful process that brought healing to a bitterly angry and divided nation.

At one of those truth and reconciliation trials a white police officer confessed to a black woman that he had shot her son at point-blank range. He and his partners then partied while they burned the son's body, turning it over and over until it was totally consumed.

Eight years later this same officer returned with his partners and seized her husband. They forced her to watch as they bound him on top of a woodpile and burned him alive. The last words she heard from her husband were, "Forgive them."

Now this white police officer faced this wife and mother and waited for her response. When the judge asked the woman what she wanted she said,

> "I want three things: First, I want this officer to take me to the spot where they burned my son so that I can gather the ashes and bury them properly.
>
> Second, I want this officer to come to my home twice a month so that I can be a mother to him since he took my child.

The Step of Knowledge

Third, I would like him to know that he is forgiven by God and by me and I would like to embrace him now, here, so that he knows my forgiveness is real.

The police officer fainted.

Someone began singing amazing grace and the entire court joined in" (From South African Truth and Reconciliation Committee Reports).

It is a mirror image of what we Christ followers have experienced with God.

**If we confess our sins, he is faithful and just
and will forgive us our sins and purify
us from all unrighteousness.
1 John 1:9**

Thousands of former police and government officials submitted to these commissions, confessing their torture and murder and robbery and abuse of black South Africans and on the basis of that pubic confession were forgiven and given amnesty. I am not aware of anything like this ever happening on such a large scale outside of Christ, for *"In him we have redemption through his blood, the forgiveness of sins, in accordance with the riches of God's grace"* (Ephesians 1:7), and *"because of his great love for us, God, who is rich in mercy, made us alive with Christ even when we were dead in transgressions—it is by grace you have been saved"* (Ephesians 2:4-5).

> "A humble Christian has and can do
> and knows more and better than
> an un-Christian philosopher."
> -Peter Lange

Seven Stone Steps

**Do not think of yourself more highly than you
ought, but rather think of yourself
with sober judgment.
Romans 12:3**

In addition, this knowledge that God commands in the words of Peter is the knowledge of humility and gentleness in a world focused on self promotion and pride, frequently employing abrasive efforts to have our way with little regard for others. Such knowledge is vital for spiritual health because, *"humility and the fear of the LORD bring wealth and honor and life"* (Proverbs 22:4).

So, knowledge is
- Knowing God's grace, mercy, wisdom, power and authority.
- Knowing God's rich plan for our salvation which includes justification, redemption and imputation.
- Knowing of the scarlet thread of Christ's sacrifice that unites all 66 books of the Bible and draws history itself into a unified whole.
- Knowing our personal culpability and great need for mercy; our proper role as a servant; our solid hope for tomorrow and eternity.
- Knowing God's imperative to us all for compassion, kindness, forbearance and love.

"Add to your faith . . . knowledge."

**I count all things to be loss, because
of the excellency of the knowledge
of Christ Jesus my Lord.
Philippians 3:8**

The Step of Knowledge

"I have taken much pains to know everything that was esteemed worth knowing among men; but with all my disquisitions and reading, nothing now remains with me, at the close of life, but this passage of Saint Paul: *'It is a faithful saying, and worthy of all acceptation, that Jesus Christ came into the world to save sinners;'* to this I cleave, and herein I find rest."
-John Selden, scholar and jurist

Chapter Five

The Step of Self-Control

"It is not the mountain we conquer,
but ourselves."
-Edmund Hillary, first man to climb Mt. Everest

**Every athlete exercises self-control in all things.
They do it to receive a perishable wreath, but
we an imperishable.
1 Corinthian 9:25 (ESV)**

In this passage from Peter's second letter, in which he lists seven virtues to be diligently added to our faith, self-control is the midway point between faith and love. This self-control he mentions is the Greek word <u>egkrateia</u> (eg-krat'-i-ah) which describes the sort of self-control that is associated with temperance or self-restraint. It is the self control that denies inordinate and inappropriate pleasures. It is primarily the self-control of appetites and it is a word that implies the kind of strength that masters a craving or lust, or overcomes a fear. Egkrateia is the tough determination to resist overeating, spending unwisely, drinking to excess, sex outside of marriage, etc. It is also the kind of self-control that allows us to continue a difficult or frightening assignment. *"For this very reason, make every effort to add to your faith . . . self-control."*

This topic is no stranger to Scripture. Personal restraint is a theme that begins in the second chapter of the Bible when God tells Adam, *"You are free to eat from any tree in the garden; but you must not eat from the tree of the knowledge of good and evil"* (Genesis 2:17). Adam was assigned great liberty to live as he desired in the Garden, but he was carefully and clearly instructed to control any desire to eat the fruit of that one specific tree. *"You must not. You must control that impulse."*

Seven Stone Steps

God did not say that He would prevent Adam from doing so. He did not build a fence around the tree or chain attack dogs to it. He implied that the tree was there and available but that Adam was charged with the responsibility to exercise self-control and thereby avoid eating that one particular fruit. Self-control. Control of, and by, myself. Egkrateia.

But there was more, much more. In the process of time God commanded His people to abstain from eating pork and shellfish and other specific foods. He commanded them to abstain from marrying foreign women and from sex outside of marriage. He commanded them to absolutely avoid any temptation to worship pagan gods. And all of those commands required self-control because God never removed the temptation, he simply commanded egkrateia.

> "There never did and never will exist
> anything permanently noble and excellent
> in character that was a stranger to
> exercise of resolute self-denial."
> -Walter Scott

For God gave us a spirit, not of fear, but of power and love and self-control.
2 Timothy 1:7

The problem with self-control is that it is notoriously weak and not to be trusted. Willpower alone is a scandalously unreliable resource as we see every year with New Year's resolutions. People solemnly vow to lose weight, stop smoking, pay down their debt, and watch less TV and dozens of other commendable efforts. Unfortunately, when those resolutions are supported only by raw self-discipline they seldom lead on to permanent success. Resolve without some source of empowerment is a very weak thing.

The Step of Self-Control

Serious self-control requires an accurate and well established self-image. This is not the self-image of physical beauty or athletic ability or academic accomplishment. It is not the self-image promoted by the popular advocates of self-esteem. Self-control requires the motivation and power that comes from seeing ourselves as God sees us, or as Paul says, *"think of yourself with sober judgment, in accordance with the measure of faith God has given you"* (Romans 12:3). It is the self-image that is associated with understanding that we Christ followers are actually adopted children of God. *"How great is the love the Father has lavished on us, that we should be called children of God! And that is what we are"* (1 John 3:1). It is not a self-image of privilege and status but of wonder and gratitude and humility.

When Saul was king of Israel he ruled a nation of millions of people. He had been appointed by God and should have grasped the magnitude and the significance of the task he had been assigned as well as the power behind it. Further he was the biggest man in the entire nation (1 Samuel 9:2), a head taller than anyone else.

When God ordered Saul to utterly destroy the Amalekites and all of their possessions, he had been given all of the required resources, both physically and spiritually. He was a big man with a big job from a big God, and his resources were not within himself but from the sovereign, good, wise God.

But Saul compromised in his appointed task and returned home with their King Agag and great flocks and herds of animals. It is a familiar passage in Scripture in which the prophet Samuel chastises Saul for his disobedience and informs him that God has thereby rejected him as King of Israel. *"Obedience is better than sacrifice"* (1 Samuel 15:22).

Many have opined that Saul was too arrogant and thought too much of himself and thereby fell into that disobedience.

Seven Stone Steps

Eugene Peterson sees it differently, "It was not that Saul thought too much of himself . . . but that he thought too little . . . that he was unaware of the importance of all that God had entrusted him" (Living the Message).

Saul's lack of self-control was exposed when he led the army of Israel against the Philistines, and Saul, the biggest man in all Israel, surrendered to his personal fears and sent the teenaged David to do his fighting against Goliath. He displayed his lack of self-control in his later behaviors with David . . . throwing his spear at him in anger, chasing him in the wilderness and seeking to kill David, who Saul knew to be God's chosen vessel.

Saul's self-image was wrong; it was too small. He failed to see that he had been appointed to a major position in the kingdom of God and therefore had an obligation to carry out those responsibilities to the fullest. Saul did not *"think in accordance with the measure of faith God had given him."* He thought too small, right to the end when he committed a self-serving suicide.

Mordecai was quite different. You can read his story in the book of Esther where you will find him to be the wise but unpretentious uncle of the simple, courageous woman who would become Queen Esther, wife of Xerxes, King of Persia. In fact, Mordecai is honored annually at the Jewish festival of Purim, one of the five great holy days for all Jews.

Mordecai was a simple Jew in a foreign land that was not kind to Jews. He was a man without credentials, without position or reputation. He was just a poor Jew. But Mordecai saw himself big because he knew he had been chosen by God, knew the power of his God and he knew his covenant relationship with God. Mordecai was plugged into the ultimate source of power and by that he was big, genuinely big. He had a sound and strong self-image because it was rooted in his relationship with the Creator. In the end, Mordecai used that self-image to save the exiled Jewish nation through his confidence and self-control, all built on a foundation of faith and trust.

So, how is it that God sees me? I want to understand that and anchor my self image in that. Then, when I grasp that firmly it becomes the engine of motivation to exercise my self-control.

Notice that this is not "self-esteem," which is a popular but flawed concept. Love of self is never proposed in Scripture and is never profitable because it focuses on the wrong thing. It is not even remotely connected to having a sound and biblically based "self-image" as a child of God and a Prince (or Princess) in His kingdom by grace.

"Self-esteem" (self-of-steam) is vapor and mirrors built on false premises. Self-image in Christ is built on a solid Rock. *"For by the grace given me I say to every one of you: Do not think of yourself more highly than you ought, but rather think of yourself with sober judgment, in accordance with the measure of faith God has given you"* (Romans 12:3).

Self-abasement and a proper self-image meet at the cross, not at my Freudian ego. But, they do meet. And from the cross I can proceed with a strong, confident image of myself as a new person with eternal life and a personal relationship with the sovereign God, and as an actual temple of the living God. It is not about loving myself; it is about having the gift of the power of the indwelling God. It is humble confidence. Confident humility. *"Humble yourselves, therefore, under God's mighty hand, that he may lift you up in due time"* (1 Peter 5:6).

How does God see me? He sees me as a fallen being, prone to sin, but on the basis of my faith in His grace He sees me as his child. Imagine! *"How great is the love the Father has lavished on us, that we should be called children of God! And that is what we are!"* (1 John 3:1). Note that we are not children of God by birth but by adoption as a consequence of His grace and our faith.

Seven Stone Steps

If that is true I am not just a child but a prince; a son of the King. If serious self-control requires an accurate and well established self-image then I have been given the resources. My self-image is strong. I am a prince, but only because God, by grace, has adopted me into His family with all the responsibility that entails.

> "The only conquests that are permanent,
> and leave no regrets, are our
> conquests over ourselves."
> -Napoleon Bonaparte

**Like a city whose walls are broken down
is a man who lacks self-control.
Proverbs 25:28**

One of the many, fine biblical stories of self-control occurs in the 39th chapter of Genesis. Joseph is a young man who has been betrayed by his jealous and spiteful brothers and sold to dessert nomads just to get rid of him. Those nomads—Midianites—carried Joseph to Egypt and sold him as a slave.

Joseph is purchased by a senior military official named Potiphar and becomes so skilled and useful in managing his owner's household and property that he is given authority over all aspects of Potiphar's assets.

The biblical account describes Joseph as "well built and handsome." Apparently he was an attractive, masculine young man and Potiphar's wife was attracted to him sexually and openly invited him into her bed—not once but daily, for some protracted period. Through all of this Joseph resisted and controlled the normal desires of his young manhood.

It is, really, a remarkable example of self-control. There is arguably no more powerful urge for a young man than sex,

The Step of Self-Control

especially proposed, offered, enticed sex. Nevertheless, Joseph is committed to honesty and purity and in the midst of a perfect opportunity—luxurious setting, an alluring and seductive woman and constant enticement—he exercises that most difficult virtue of self-control. There was not one barrier to this immorality except Joseph's own self-control. If that was all I knew about Joseph he would still be one of my great heroes.

I read of a mother walking through the grocery store with a small child who was crying.

"Ashley, you can do this," she said, "We will be finished in just a few minutes."

The child continued to struggle and cry and the mother said, "We're almost done, Ashley. Just be patient for a few more minutes."

When they reached the checkout line the child became hysterical and the mother said, "Ashley just hold on, we'll be on the way home in a minute."

When they finally reached the parking lot an older man stopped her to say, "I wanted to compliment you on how patient you were with Ashley."

Well, the mother laughed, "The truth is that I am Ashley."

Don't miss the point here. Ashley is not the child, Ashley is the mother carrying the squalling, unreasonable child and Ashley—the mother of this difficult child—is talking to herself because she—the mother—needs self-control at that moment. She is striving for that self-control by talking to herself, "You can do this." "Be patient." "Hold on." Ashley has given up on changing the child's behavior at the moment and is rightly concentrating on her own self-control.

> "He who conquers others is strong.
> He who conquers himself is mighty."
> -Lao-Tze

Seven Stone Steps

**Better a patient man than a warrior, a man who
controls his temper than one who takes a city.
Proverbs 16:32**

David was a warrior from his youth; the youngest of eight brothers he likely had two choices for his life: either fade into servility or persist in his determination to be independent. It is clear that he chose the latter. He chose to be an independent servant of God, obedient to his father and family but always with a higher purpose.

As a youth David tended his father's sheep, a lonely and sometimes dangerous occupation. Sheep are particular delicacies for large predators and they are notoriously stupid. David was their only defender. At some point during this tender age his flock was raided by at least one lion and one bear and in both of those cases David confronted the beasts and dispatched them with little more than his bare hands. Clearly, David was a fighter.

While still a young man, he visited his brothers at the battle front and volunteered to take on the Philistine giant Goliath. It is an amazing story. Here a dedicated and confident teen volunteers for a frightful challenge that has already been declined by the biggest man in all of Israel, King Saul. It is an inconceivable match but David accepts the challenge and wins the fight, killing Goliath and removing his head just to be sure. David was a warrior and driven to win.

After this impressive event, Saul appoints David as an officer in his army and David goes on to slay thousands of the enemy. Because of this and the fame it created, Saul was murderously jealous and David fled to the wilderness where he was constantly harassed by Saul who wanted to eliminate this young, popular warrior whom God had chosen to be King. Saul was cruel and vengeful and aggressive toward David. He was determined to hunt him down and eliminate him and David knew this well.

At one point in this period of Israel's history, David was hiding from Saul's forces in a cave in the wilderness. David knew two things: that Saul was God's appointed King and that Saul was determined to kill him.

As it happened, Saul entered the cave to relieve himself. David realized that he was being presented with the perfect opportunity to creep out from the dark recesses and dispatch the king as he was otherwise occupied. It would have ended David's life as a fugitive and installed him on the throne of Israel. It was the answer to all of his immediate problems. Even David's companions encouraged him, saying, "This is the day the Lord spoke of when He said, 'I will give your enemy into your hands.'" It was a perfect solution.

But David responded—with a major display of egkrateia—that he would not harm the man who was currently God's anointed ruler of Israel. So David crept forward in that cave and when he was within reach he simply sliced off a corner of Saul's garment so that he could later display that piece of fabric as a testimony of his loyalty to the king, the anointed ruler, despite Saul's bitter and unwarranted persecution.

It was a heroic display of self-control for a man who was a passionate warrior. *"Better a patient man than a warrior, a man who controls his temper than one who takes a city"* (Proverbs 16:32).

It is an encouraging example for us who would like to choke our neighbor's barking dog or tamper with that incessantly speeding teenager's car, or fry our neighbor's stereo or flatten the boss's tires.

Seven Stone Steps

Self-control. Self-restraint. Self-discipline. But always by the power of the Holy Spirit who reminds us that our goal and desire as adopted children of God is to please Him. *"For this very reason, make every effort to add to your faith . . . self-control."*

> "I count him braver who overcomes his
> desires than him who conquers his enemies;
> for the hardest victory is the victory over self."
> -Aristotle

**Every athlete exercises self-control in all things.
They do it to receive a perishable wreath,
but we an imperishable.
1 Corinthians 9:25 (ESV)**

My brother John was three years older, big and self-confident. When he was sixteen he secured a job for the summer as a camp counselor on Cape Cod, a long drive from our house. My overworked Dad drove him there on the appointed Saturday and within a few more days John was laid off from his job because the camper enrollments that summer were light. Calling home for a ride was not an option. Mom didn't drive and Dad was working. Together they had raised a family through the depression and knew that work could usually be found with enough effort.

So John packed a rucksack and began the walk into town to look for work. When he got to a small diner/motel complex the gruff owner said, "Sure, I have work but you won't do it." But since no one liked a challenge better than John, his remark was a sure invitation to accomplish whatever was needed.

The work, as it turned out was simply to take eight or ten trash cans, way out there on the back of the property, to the dump in the owners' truck. It seemed pretty benign until John got the truck up close to the cans and realized they were filled with rotting, stinking garbage and overflowing with maggots in the summer heat. Maggots everywhere, flowing like little white waterfalls down the sides of the cans and over the ground. It was a maggot metropolis and John's job was to move those cans onto the truck, then to the dump, a job that required very close contact with a lot of maggots—maggots on your clothes, in your shoes and all over your hands, arms and legs. Maggot heaven and a world of stink, but—a potential job!

It was a challenge made for my brother, who badly needed a job and who loved a challenge, so he stifled his revulsion, loaded the cans and drove them to the dump. At the dump he emptied the maggot-mess and returned to the diner/motel where he washed the cans and truck and reported for more work. That episode of self-control earned him the respect of the owner and a very nice job for the rest of that summer.

John's self-control was admirable and it is a nice, practical example but it is different from the self-control that Peter commands in our theme verse. Peter is insisting on a self-control that is grounded in personal faith and trust in a living God who is sovereign, wise and good. Will power is good, but trust in a personal God is infinitely better. Years later, as a successful executive, father of six, and brother in Christ, John would have told you all of that himself.

> "Teach me to see that Christ does not desire me to live in self-confidence in my own strength but gives me the law of the Spirit of life to enable me to obey."
> -*The Valley of Vision*
> (A Book of Puritan Prayers)

Seven Stone Steps

**That is why, for Christ's sake,
I delight in weaknesses, in insults,
in hardships, in persecutions, in difficulties.
For when I am weak, then I am strong.
2 Corinthians 12:10**

Chapter Six

The Step of Perseverance

*"Perseverance is persistence
that results in triumph."
-Anonymous*

**For this very reason, make every effort
to add to your faith . . . perseverance.
2 Peter 1:6**

Several generations of American children grew up with the story of "The Little Engine that Could." It was a purely secular story that emphasized the value of perseverance in the face of what seems to be an impossible task.

It is a simple story about a small railroad engine that was designed for the light work of switching cars in the station yard. One morning a long train of freight cars asked a big engine, built for hard work, to take it over the hill but the big engine said, "I can't; the hill is too big for me." The freight train asked other engines but they all declined because they thought they could not pull that huge train up the long hill. Finally the train asked the little switch engine and he said, "I think I can."

So the little engine hitched up the long freight cars and started up the long, hard hill. As it went, the little engine kept on puffing and saying to himself, "I think I can. I think I can. I think I can." It was a long hard pull, very near the limits of that little engine's strength, but he never quit, and he constantly reminded himself, "I think I can. I think I can," until he crested the hill and went down the backside saying, "I thought I could. I thought I could. I thought I could." His perseverance was determination that resulted in triumph.

Seven Stone Steps

This virtue of perseverance that God commands through Peter's words is surely one of the most unpopular of all virtues. It means that we are commanded to press on despite all of the unpleasant circumstances that intervene and just keep on enduring in the right direction. Through uncertainty, disappointment, doubt, fear and anxiety we are commanded to persevere. It is not a virtue we can exercise very long by sheer willpower, like the little engine, but it is a virtue we can sustain by the ongoing assistance of the Holy Spirit.

So with this command to persevere—to persevere in the right direction—we know we can energize that perseverance with the only inexhaustible source: God Himself in the form of His indwelling Spirit.

The word that Peter uses here is the Greek <u>hupomone</u> (hoopo-monay), which is a compound of two words roughly meaning to abide under or to continue through. It is a word used almost 50 times in the New Testament as either a verb or a noun. And it is variously translated into English as "perseverance," "patience," "steadfastness," or "patient endurance."

In the end, it is not a difficult concept. We all understand the simple idea of "keeping on, keeping on." It is a challenge we have faced since grammar school with eating our spinach, doing our homework, writing that final term paper, mowing the lawn, finding a job, finishing an assignment, a career and a life. Vance Havner, the wonderful preacher and author from Jugtown, NC said it simply, "It is not enough to stare up the steps—we must step up the stairs." And in a life-scope view of perseverance, Dr. Havner often said that he prayed he would "Get home before dark"; that he would persevere to the end of his God-appointed days without falling into moral or spiritual darkness. *"For this very reason, make every effort to add to your faith . . . perseverance."*

> "In His infinite wisdom, God allows trials in order to develop perseverance in us, and to cause us to fix our hopes on the glory that is yet to be revealed . . . Our faith and perseverance can grow only under the pain of trial."
> —Jerry Bridges

You have heard of Job's perseverance and have seen what the Lord finally brought about. The Lord is full of compassion and mercy.
James 5:11

The single most brilliant example of perseverance in all of Scripture and, for that matter, in all of known literature, is the story of a man named Job. Note here that Job was persevering—hupomone—even though he was decidedly not always patient, tolerant or uncomplaining. In fact, he was none of those, but he was, through it all, a man of perseverance. It is his endearing quality. James reminds us of "Job's perseverance" in James 5:11.

We know a lot about Job. We know that he was so righteous in his behavior that God actually bragged about him to Satan. We know that he was a happy and wealthy patriarch with vast holdings and a beloved family. We know that God chose to test his faith and his trust by removing all of his personal comforts: wealth, children, marital joy and, finally, his health. In a very short time Job was reduced to an impoverished wretch, covered with boils, rejected by his bitter wife and grieving for his dead children. Job's losses are difficult to imagine, but they were specifically designed by the hand of God to remove any apathy Job might have accumulated about the greatness and sovereignty of the One he worshipped, and to energize his faith and trust with fresh understanding. And we know that in the midst of this personal tragedy he had moments of towering faith, *"Though he slay me, yet will I hope in him"* (Job 13:15), and *"I know that my Redeemer lives"* (Job 19:25).

Seven Stone Steps

But we also know the dark side of Job's perseverance. We know that during Job's travail he was angry, petulant, fearful, doubting, sarcastic, self-righteous, anxious and critical. Job was not a perfect victim. He wavered and flailed about like any troubled person, but somehow he always managed to find that confident trust that God was in it, that God had a purpose, that Job was an instrument for God's glory. He is a model of perseverance, despite his many and obvious flaws.

So we learn from Job that we can persevere, even in the most trying circumstances. We learn that Job's flaws—and ours—are covered by God's mercy and compassion. We learn that perseverance is not mere persistence but persistence to the point of victory. Without some final, spiritual victory there is no perseverance. In the end, Job experienced great victory and reward from God.

"By perseverance the snail reached the ark."
-Charles Spurgeon

**May the Lord direct your hearts into God's love and Christ's perseverance.
2 Thessalonians 3:5**

One of my dear friends, along with his wife, spent 20 years as missionaries to Stone Age people in the southern lowlands of Papua New Guinea. In the pursuit of a clear understanding of this virtue of perseverance, it is helpful to consider the magnitude of this task which has been repeated hundreds of times by thousands of missionaries on every continent. The basic task is to deliver a printed Bible in the local language, and to teach the literacy required to read and understand it. Accomplishing this goal is a challenge that will demand at least a 20 year commitment to achieve and a lifetime of long term follow-up. Persistence to the point of triumph (perseverance) is absolutely required.

First, they must be schooled in the art and science of linguistics, a learning challenge that can require years of preparation. Then there is the daunting task of raising financial support which normally requires a year or two of tedious travel in the U.S. to solicit contributors who will faithfully and regularly donate to their work.

An appropriate people-group must be identified and contacted and some sort of agreement must be reached that will allow the missionary to live and work in their area. There is the strenuous work of assembling the necessary supplies, locating and moving to a location that is often accessible only by small airplane, boat, and/or foot.

Now the language work can begin. The local language will not have a written form and the vocabulary and syntax will certainly be new and often confusing. How do I make that sound that is so much a part of their spoken language when there is no such sound in my own native language? And how do I learn and catalogue the extensive vocabulary that must be acquired before I can begin to translate? How would they say "grace," "justification," "crucifixion," or "salvation"?

It is a years-long process and then . . . how do I represent all of those sounds and words with letters on a printed page? And how do I begin the formidable job of teaching a primitive people to correlate printed symbols to spoken words, what we call reading?

In the end it is a process that needs great reliance on the power of God to provide the persistence to continue day-by-day. It is keeping on with keeping on year after year in the face of tribal warfare, sickness, epidemics, drought, floods, fires, famines and government interference, as well as personal discouragement and fear and anxiety. It is twenty years of persistence, doggedness and determination.

And when the project is complete (if it is completed) there comes a day when printed Bibles in the local language are delivered to a people who are now able to read God's revealed Word in their native tongue. There will be a celebration and a feast and rejoicing because these faithful ambassadors have persisted to the final moment of triumph. It is the very essence of perseverance. *"For this very reason, make every effort to add to your faith . . . perseverance."*

> "Perseverance is more than endurance.
> It is endurance combined with absolute
> assurance and certainty that what we are
> looking for is going to happen."
> -Oswald Chambers

**You need to persevere so that when you have done the will of God, you will receive what he has promised.
Hebrews 10:36**

The second chapter of Luke's gospel tells the story of Jesus' birth and early years up to about age twelve. Part of that story includes the subplot of an obscure man who is a model of perseverance for us. His name was Simeon and Luke mentions him as follows.

> **In Jerusalem at the time, there was a man, Simeon by name, a good man, a man who lived in the prayerful expectancy of help for Israel. And the Holy Spirit was on him. The Holy Spirit had shown him that he would see the Messiah of God before he died. Led by the Spirit, he entered the Temple. As the parents of the child Jesus brought him in to carry out the rituals of the Law, Simeon took him into his arms and blessed God:**

The Step of Perseverance

> **"God, you can now release your servant; release me in peace as you promised. With my own eyes I've seen your salvation; it's now out in the open for everyone to see: A God-revealing light to the non-Jewish nations, and of glory for your people Israel" (Luke 2:25-32, The Message).**

This is all that we know about Simeon, so the story requires some speculation regarding the details. But it appears that Simeon was an older man who had faithfully waited for Messiah on the basis of his knowledge of biblical prophecy and a personal promise he had received from the Holy Spirit. He had persisted through all the turmoil of Roman occupation, religious squabbles among Pharisees and Sadducees and numerous minor Jewish sects, and through all of the normal trials of life, always waiting expectantly to see the promised Messiah, the greatest event in all history.

Simeon waited. He spent day after day walking to the temple and waiting with confident expectation. He persisted.

And then after years of persisting, Simeon rejoiced in that triumphant moment when he held the Son of God in his arms. Imagine that! Imagine feeling the soft humanity of The One who had come to take away the sins of the world. Simeon's persistence reached that high standard of perseverance when it was crowned with a triumphal conclusion.

> "God knows our situation; He will not judge us as if we had no difficulties to overcome. What matters is the sincerity and perseverance of our will to overcome them."
> –C.S. Lewis

Seven Stone Steps

> **Therefore, since we are surrounded by such a great cloud of witnesses, let us throw off everything that hinders and the sin that so easily entangles, and let us run with perseverance the race marked out for us.**
> **Hebrews 12:1**

Good advice. Consider the great cloud of people who have demonstrated perseverance in the past. Our perseverance in faith is so important to God that He inspired the writer of Hebrews to devote an entire chapter (chapter 11) to the heroes of faith As we think about perseverance, consider Noah, Abraham, Isaac, Jacob, Moses, Joshua, Rahab, Gideon, David, Samuel, and of course, Job. Meditate on the hardships and trials they endured and on the persistence and the final triumph that qualifies them as those who persevered. The Christian life consists of spiritual conflict and warfare, and perseverance plays a vital part in our success.

But be sure to note this: for many of those men and women the point of triumph was the moment of death. They persisted through punishing circumstances with faith that God had a purpose for it all, and yet for some there was no final triumph until they were able to face the object of their faith and hear those coveted words, *"Well done, good and faithful servant!"*

And so that leaves us with the challenge to persist in godliness, always looking for that moment of triumph: a new believer, a repentant heart, a healed relationship, a child grown to maturity, a teaching or sermon well done, or a personal victory over sin. Persistence to the point of triumph.

For two winters, my wife Fran and I vacationed in a condo loaned by a generous young friend. It was a lovely place on the top floor of an eight story building and many times we chose to walk up those stairs rather than use the elevator. On some

The Step of Perseverance

occasions after a long day, it was more than we really felt like doing and we would call out the fractions as we climbed. "One eighth." "Two eighths." "Five sixteenths." There were times when we felt like counting each step—all 144 of them—and I think of that as a simple parable of perseverance. As long as we kept moving up we were persisting, enduring, but when we reached that landing on the eighth floor we could rightly claim the virtue of perseverance, because at that level we had "persisted to the point of triumph."

But there is one example of perseverance that surely exceeds all others and that is the perseverance of Jesus Christ in His assignment to gather all the sins of all men unto Himself and become the perfect sacrifice.

Jesus had to persist through years of menial labor as a village tradesman and then through three exhausting years of constant ministry to demanding crowds and bickering, slow-witted disciples. He had to persist through the agony of prayer in Gethsemane and then the arrest, trial, beatings and insults, and death by crucifixion, during which His own Father turned away in disgust at the sins of the world He carried with him to the cross, and then burial in a dark tomb.

He persisted through it all and on that third day He stunned the world with His moment of triumph and for that He will always be the Chief of all perseverance—the risen sacrificial Lamb of God who takes away the sins of the world for all who believe.

> "Christ the Lord is ris'n today, Alleluia!
> Sons of men and angels say, Alleluia!
> Raise your joys and triumphs high, Alleluia!
> Sing, ye heav'ns, and earth reply, Alleluia!"
> -Charles Wesley

Seven Stone Steps

**As you know, we consider blessed those
who have persevered.
James 5:11**

Chapter Seven

The Step of Godliness

"True godliness does not turn men out of the world but enables them to live better in it and excites their endeavors to mend it."
-William Penn

His divine power has given us everything we need for life and godliness through our knowledge of him who called us by his own glory and goodness.
2 Peter 1:3

It is a strange command, really, this command for us who have been declared by God to be fallen creatures and corrupt beings to now be instructed to add the virtue of "godliness" to our conduct. It's not too difficult to understand a decree for goodness or knowledge or self-control, but—godliness? Are we really obligated to develop behaviors that are godly in nature? It is strange and it bears some attention since it is, after all, a pretty clear command and this is not the only place it occurs. *"For this very reason, make every effort to add to your faith . . . godliness."*

One thing that makes this command more comprehensible is the promise in Peter's preamble before it, that by God's own glory and goodness He has given us great and precious promises that enable us to participate in the divine nature. Really? Me participate in divinity? But this is not a formula that lends itself to much analysis. It is a simple statement by the Sovereign God that His personal glory and goodness are the source of promises and those promises—in some undefined way—enable us to develop a nature that has elements of godliness. There is no logical explanation of why or how all of this is true. It just is. It is one more occasion for faith. *"For this very reason, make every effort to add to your faith . . . godliness."*

But once again we are confronted with the challenge of understanding just what this "godliness" looks like. The Pharisees practiced something they considered to be godliness and Jesus mocked and rebuked them. Those who withdraw from the world in order to cultivate their personal holiness practice something they assume is godliness but it is clearly not the biblical variety that openly connects with the fallen world system in order to bring light. There have been many systems and definitions of godliness but the godliness that Peter commands in this passage is unique.

> "Godliness is more than Christian character.
> It covers the totality of the Christian life
> and provides the foundation upon which
> Christian character is built."
> -Jerry Bridges

But you, man of God, flee from all this, and pursue righteousness, godliness, faith, love, endurance and gentleness.
1 Timothy 6:11

The Greek word that Paul uses here, <u>eusebeia</u> (yoo-seb'-i-a) — is found 15 times in the New Testament. It has the general meaning of reverence or piety, and in this context it is certain that Peter's meaning is reverence for the one, true God, who is the topic of the entire Bible, and for the Bible itself since it is God's personal statement to humanity. Eusebeia could be used in the context of reverence for an esteemed superior or a parent and, actually, that is the case here, although the parent involved in this case is our heavenly one.

Godliness in this context is the deliberate and conscious respect and worship of the One who loves us and has adopted all those who have embraced His salvation and lordship. This

The Step of Godliness

godliness is not a form of extreme moralism, but rather, a deep adoration of God which motivates behaviors that are pleasing to Him. If we see Him as He is—supreme, sovereign, gracious, merciful, patient, loving, all-powerful, compassionate and wise—godliness is not some form of super spirituality but a natural response to what is.

Consider Job. Job was a normal man in the midst of a normal but affluent life. He was a pious man, a righteous man and we know that because God, Himself, said that Job was *"blameless and upright, a man who fears God and turns away from evil"* (Job 1:8). So, Job was a guy you would see every week in church and about whom you would hear and see nothing but good. But even Job could use a lesson in godliness and that is the topic of that long and sometimes tedious book. If you skip to the closing you will see Job's renewed and strengthened "godliness" (eusebeia) in his exclamation that *"I know that you can do all things; no plan of yours can be thwarted . . . My ears have heard of you but now my eyes have seen you."* We know that Job never did actually see God physically because Scripture is clear that no one has ever done that, but the eyes of Job's heart had been opened in a new and fresh way, so that his reverence and admiration were magnified. It was a leap in Job's godliness which led Job to new levels of virtue. *"For this very reason, make every effort to add to your faith . . . godliness."*

> "The practice of godliness is an exercise
> or discipline that focuses upon God.
> From this Godward attitude arises the
> character and conduct that we
> usually think of as godliness."
> –Jerry Bridges

Have nothing to do with godless myths and old wives' tales; rather, train yourself to be godly for physical training is of some value, but godliness has value for all things, holding promise for both the present life and the life to come.
1 Timothy 4:7-8

There is a two-dimensional quality to this godliness: it begins with a disciplined reverence for God and that reverence, when it has plumbed the depths of God's magnificence and power and grace and compassion, produces the behaviors that we associate with godliness. The truly godly people you have known and admired did not simply act out some lifestyle with self-discipline. They first *"trained themselves in godliness"* through the mental and spiritual discipline of knowing God to the very limits of what is possible. Knowing God—in depth—is just the first step in this virtue of godliness, but it is an essential first step. Without that, there is no true godliness, only secular morality.

Richard Wurmbrand was born into a Jewish family in Bucharest, Romania, in 1909. As an adolescent he was sent to Russia to study Marxism in Moscow, but he secretly returned to Bucharest the next year. In 1936 he married his wife Sabrina, and in 1938 they both became believers in Jesus Christ as their messiah and were dedicated followers of Him.

Richard and Sabrina joined the Anglican Mission to The Jews, and he was ordained as a minister. In that capacity he ministered to his countrymen and to the occupying Russian communist soldiers, testifying to them of God's love and their need of saving faith in Jesus Christ. In a short time, Pastor Wurmbrand's ministry was forced underground to avoid persecution from the communist dictators and in 1948 he was arrested and imprisoned. By this time Richard Wurmbrand had trained himself greatly in the godliness of biblical knowledge and virtue. He had become a student of the Bible and a disciplined follower of Jesus Christ. *"Train yourself to be godly."*

During 14 years in oppressive communist prisons he endured unspeakable torture and deprivation. Three of those years were spent in solitary confinement in a cell that was underground and without light or windows. During that time, he was alone, in the dark, with God as his only resource. It is the very circumstance that desperately cries for prior training in godliness, eusebeia . . . a deep affection and adoration of the One True God who alone controls all things and who loves His children in ways and in places that we cannot understand.

During those three years of absolute isolation, Wurmbrand avoided the depression and self-pity that would have consumed a less godly person by employing the following routine: Each night he would mentally compose an entire sermon and when it was complete he would deliver that sermon into the darkness. And when he had delivered it, as if to an audience of thousands, he would consign key points of the sermon to a mental file. Later, when he was released, he published a book of those sermons titled, "With God in Solitary Confinement."

How was Pastor Wurmbrand able to do that when so many others were broken psychologically and spiritually by the experience? Because he had made every effort to *"add to his faith godliness"* and in that stinking prison he found that *"godliness has value for all things, holding promise for both the present life and the life to come."*

Paul felt so strongly about this principle that he reminded his beloved young friend Timothy of the positive benefits of physical training as an encouragement to godliness training. Remember here that Paul and Timothy were well acquainted with physical training. They lived in a society that was dominated by Greek culture that revered the human body in a way eerily similar to

Seven Stone Steps

America in the late 20th century, where people routinely joined clubs and spas to buff their abs and carve their profile. They did the same in ancient Athens and all through the world that Paul and Timothy knew. Gymnasiums were a big element of Greek culture.

Timothy would have been well aware of this Greek custom and when Paul advised him to *"train himself,"* using the Greek word gumnazo, (goom-nad'-zo) (from which we get our English word "gymnasium"), Timothy would have immediately made the connection between physical training and spiritual training. They both require serious effort and deliberate exertion. Just as those who want to buff their physical bodies need to stress and sweat, those who would *"train (gumnazo) themselves in godliness"* must do the same in a spiritual and mental way. No pain, no gain; no effort, no progress.

Further, this training in our knowledge of God comes primarily through an understanding of His Word found in the Bible. You can recognize the magnificence of God in nature, but you cannot discern His character and purpose without a clear understanding of what He has told us in those 66 books. You don't have to graduate from seminary, but there is no alternative to the Bible itself for growth in godliness. Study the book of Isaiah. Read the book of Job and especially chapters 36-41. Examine Psalms 19 and 139. Make your own search, but *"train yourself in godliness"* by discovering the majesty, perfection, splendor, sovereignty, wisdom, mercy, compassion and grace of God in all its dimensions.

> "Wash out your ego every once in a while,
> as cleanliness is next to godliness not just in
> body but in humility as well."
> -Anonymous

The Step of Godliness

Since everything will be destroyed in this way, what kind of people ought you to be? You ought to live holy and godly lives as you look forward to the day of God and speed its coming.
2 Peter 3:11-12

So this Greek eusebeia that Peter uses here and which we translate as "godliness" has a primary meaning of reverence or respect and carries the certain implication that such reverence and respect will produce results. Any child who truly respects his parents will treat them in predictable, honorable ways, especially when those children have matured to an age at which they understand the true meaning of respect. Eric Metaxas, in his biography of Dietrich Bonhoeffer, the WWII German pastor and martyr, describes Dietrich's father as a strong figure whom the eight children deeply loved and says this, "His children loved and respected him in a way that made them eager to gain his approval."

Their mother, Paula Bonhoeffer, told her children, "There is no place for false piety or bogus religiosity in our home." Dietrich would later apply that same principle to his Christian life as his deep personal reverence for God led him to openly disobey the Nazi government in his role as a pastor, challenging the German people from the pulpit to something more than what he called "cheap grace." For that he was eventually martyred by a Nazi hanging. Eusebeia.

Military personnel who respect their leaders will follow them with great loyalty even in difficult circumstances because they know that respect is more than an emotion. Occasionally—and only occasionally—there is a military leader of whom his men say, "We would have followed him to the gates of hell." David's men knew him intimately from their many long struggles together. They so respected and revered him that when he mused aloud about his thirst for the water from a particular well in Bethlehem they fought their way through the Philistine defenses just to retrieve a jug of that water. Eusebeia. It is a well-informed reverence that moves us to appropriate behavior.

In both of these examples the children and the soldiers knew their leaders intimately and what they knew motivated them to extraordinary deference and obedience.

The sequence of this is important. Intimate knowledge first and then grateful obedience as the natural result of that knowledge. Eusebeia.

In the end it is always good and appropriate to remember the cross where the creator and sustainer of all things, the purest, strongest, most gracious and virtuous being who ever existed, stooped to carry the burden and the penalty of my sin and yours.

He was nailed to that cross with three great iron spikes driven though His hands and feet, but it was not those spikes that held Him there. That was His mercy and grace and love. And when we know that, and appreciate that, and apply that, the simple virtues of godliness flow more freely.

> "True godliness leaves the world convinced
> beyond a shadow of a doubt, that the
> only explanation for you is Jesus Christ, to
> whose eternally unchanging and altogether
> adequate 'I AM!' your heart has learned to
> say with unshatterable faith, 'Thou art!'"
> -Major Ian Thomas

His divine power has given us everything we need for life and godliness through our knowledge of him who called us by his own glory and goodness.
2 Peter 1:3

Chapter Eight
The Step of Brotherly Kindness

> "The greatest thing a man can do for
> his Heavenly Father is to be kind to
> some of His other children."
> -Henry Drummond

**For this very reason, make every effort to add to
your faith . . . brotherly kindness
2 Peter 1:5, 7**

If you follow the trajectory of these seven virtues that we have been examining from 2 Peter 1:5-7 you will see that there is a steady upward trend from:

- That robust general "goodness" which can be understood as vigorous moral excellence at its best,
- to spiritual (biblical) "knowledge" that informs and directs that goodness,
- to "self-control" that disciplines the pursuit of that goodness,
- to "perseverance" that is a commitment to finish the course of goodness,
- to "godliness" that is a deep reverence and adoration of the triune God as the wellspring of goodness,
- to "brotherly kindness" that is the application of that goodness to others . . . and finally (as we will see in the next chapter),
- to that "love" which is the ultimate manifestation of God-inspired and God-empowered goodness in our life.

So here we want to examine this sixth virtue in Peter's list that is most commonly translated "brotherly kindness." And, in fact, those two words are a sound rendition of the original

Seven Stone Steps

Greek <u>philadelphia</u> which is itself a combination of two words, one for affection and one for brotherly. Every school kid learns that the city of Philadelphia is the "city of brotherly love."

So this virtue that follows godliness is a virtue of kindness to others, all others. It is loving other people in a way that transcends my personal agenda so as to produce acts of charity. And it is reasonable advice because there is a great need for simple kindnesses of all sizes and shapes. But despite that certain need there is a serious flaw in human nature that ignores the needs of others and attends to our own selfish desires.

It is for this very reason that Peter takes the time and space to instruct us in this passage, *"for this very reason, make every effort to add to your faith . . . brotherly kindness."* You might think that intelligent, educated people would understand the need for charity and perform those kindnesses based on some moral logic, but history proves otherwise. We need the knowledge, the self-control, the perseverance and the godliness that are the result of a personal relationship with God to bring forth this brotherly kindness. Education and culture alone are not sufficient. History is filled with ugly examples of educated, intelligent and talented people who were also harsh, violent and cruel. Think Stalin, Genghis Khan, Pol Pot and Hitler. Without those antecedents that Peter lists, brotherly kindness is nearly unknown.

> "I think one's feelings waste themselves in words; they ought all to be distilled into actions which bring results."
> -Florence Nightingale

Keep on loving each other as brothers.
Hebrews 13:1

The territory of Crimea is located on a peninsula on the north shore of the Black Sea just south of the Ukraine. It is one of those unfortunate pieces of real estate that has been the scene of interminable war for centuries because it lies at the boundary of opposing cultures and religions. Today it is an autonomous republic within the country of Ukraine.

In 1853 the great Ottoman Empire based in Constantinople collapsed. Because this collapse created a vacuum of power in the Balkans, England and several European kingdoms felt it was necessary to protect their interests in that area from the expanding Russian Empire. The result was what is now called the "Crimean War." At least a dozen nations took part in that bloody conflict with almost a million soldiers on each side. Casualties were appalling; nearly 400,000 men died and countless others were wounded or permanently disabled by disease and infection. It is a war best remembered for *The Charge of the Light Brigade* in which 600 British cavalry charged a Russian artillery position with 50% casualties and little or no gain. "Theirs but to do and die." (*The Charge of the Light Brigade* Alfred, Lord Tennyson.) The Crimean War was particularly ugly, even for war.

The wounded of this brutal war were simply warehoused in stinking "hospitals" where they received little attention other than the amputation of mangled limbs and dirty bandages over gaping wounds. Food and water were foul and limited. Sanitation was disgusting. Approximately 70-90% of all deaths were the result of disease: typhoid, typhus, dysentery, cholera, and rampant infection.

When she learned of these horrific conditions, Florence Nightingale, an English woman of noble birth, assembled a group of 38 women volunteers to become the first modern nursing corp. They traveled to the Ottoman Empire where the British barracks were located near present day Istanbul and began a two year stint of caring for the sick and wounded.

Seven Stone Steps

In order to grasp the "brotherly kindness" of Florence and her sisters, it is helpful to consider the conditions these cultured and privileged women would have encountered and how those conditions contrasted with their home lives. Florence herself had been born into wealth with all the privileges of abundant food, clean and warm housing, personal servants, freshly laundered clothes and sanitary water. All of the women had grown up in a culture of careful separation of men and women and socially enforced ignorance of "maleness" and all it entailed.

In the war zone they ministered daily to men who were housed in the abiding filth of neglected dead bodies, blood, vomit, diarrhea, urine, sweat and hideous wounds. It was a house of filth and deprivation with hundreds of deaths every day. Their duties involved the physically intimate work of bathing and caring for men in total contrast to the refined niceties of their backgrounds. Florence and her team purposely ignored sights and sounds and smells and cultural prohibitions that were both physically and socially revolting and shocking in the extreme in order to bring comfort to sick and dying men.

At night, when all of the doctors were sleeping, Florence walked the aisles carrying a small lamp in order to check the patients during those lonely hours of darkness. In time she came to be called "The Lady of the Lamp" and The London Times reported, "She is a 'ministering angel' without any exaggeration in these hospitals, and as her slender form glides quietly along each corridor, every poor fellow's face softens with gratitude at the sight of her. When all the medical officers have retired for the night and silence and darkness have settled down upon those miles of prostrate sick, she may be observed alone, with a little lamp in her hand, making her solitary rounds."

It was the beginning of modern nursing, and it was a work of remarkable human sacrifice and kindness over an extended period. It was so impressive that over 150 years later the name

"Florence Nightingale" personifies sacrifice and personal service. *"For this very reason, make every effort to add to your faith . . . brotherly kindness."*

> "Kindness is the inner disposition, created by the Holy Spirit, that causes us to be sensitive to the needs of others."
> -Jerry Bridges

Love the Lord your God with all your heart and with all your soul and with all your strength and with all your mind; and, love your neighbor as yourself.
Luke 10:27

One of the memorable and touching stories of the New Testament is told only by Luke in his gospel. It is a story of brotherly kindness and it is so well known that even secular organizations capitalize on it by using the name "Good Samaritan."

Surely you know this story but it is such a lovely example of philadelphia that it is worth remembering and savoring. Jesus tells this story, and He tells it immediately after being challenged by an expert in the Jewish Law who confronted Him with the question, *"Good teacher, what must I do to inherit eternal life?"* (Luke 10:29).

In response to that question Jesus asks the man what he, himself, thinks is the answer, to which the man replies, *"love God and love my neighbor"* (Luke 10:27, abbreviated). When Jesus confirms the correctness of that answer, the expert, as some experts are prone to do, can't let it go and provokes Jesus with a follow-up question, *"Who is my neighbor?"* (Luke 10:20). So that is the setting as Jesus tells the story . . .

Seven Stone Steps

A certain man was traveling from Jerusalem to Jericho, a distance of about 17 miles along a dirt road known then as "The Way of Blood" because of the routine violence there. It was good terrain for spontaneous attacks and there were plenty of thugs along the way ready to rob and injure. The English words "robbers" or "thieves" probably fall short of the full meaning of the violent criminals who physically mugged, brutalized and humiliated their victims. Indeed, the text of Jesus' story explicitly says that the man was robbed, stripped of his clothing and beaten so severely that his attackers thought him near death.

A Jewish priest came by and seeing the poor, wounded victim just crossed to the other side of the road and hurried by. This priest was a religious man, a holy man. But he was too busy with religious stuff and personal agenda, so it was inconvenient to get involved and he hurried on by. *Who is my neighbor? Who is my brother?*

Next a Levite came along—one of that class of men who assisted the priests and whose life was intimately involved in the religious worship of the temple. This Levite took a moment to look over the wounded and prostrate fellow Jew but he too was too busy and so he passed on. *"You know, if you get involved in these things there's no end to it."*

Finally there came a very different person, a Samaritan. The Samaritans were of mixed race and worshipped in their own temple on Mount Gerizim near Shechem, far to the north of Jerusalem. Their practices were an abomination to the Jews. Samaritan history is complex and murky, but at the time of Jesus the Samaritans were despised by the Jews for their racial impurity and their compromised religion. Think of Samaritans as the minority race that is considered inferior in every way by the culturally dominant Jews. Think of blacks in America a hundred years ago or Jews in Germany during the holocaust.

The Step of Brotherly Kindness

Who is my neighbor? Who is my brother? Love your neighbor as yourself.

So it is one of those spurned and disdained Samaritans who happens upon the robbed and injured Jew and this Samaritan's perspective is entirely different. Whereas the Priest and the Levite asked themselves, *"If I stop and help this man what will happen to me?"* The Samaritan asked himself *"If I don't stop and help this man what will happen to him?"* It was the right question. It still is the right question.

So the Samaritan, one of that despised racial minority considered morally and spiritually inferior by Jews, didn't hesitate to interrupt his schedule and foul his own fine clothing with mud and blood in order to help the injured Jew onto his donkey and then take him to an inn where he would be safe and receive basic care.

The Samaritan understood that his brother was anyone in need. And having that prepared heart it was perfectly natural for him to see the need and ask himself, *"What will happen to this man if I do nothing?"*

Philadelphia. Brotherly kindness. "What will happen if I do nothing?"

> "If you were arrested for kindness, would there be enough evidence to convict you?"
> -Author Unknown

> **Therefore, as God's chosen people, holy and dearly loved, clothe yourselves with compassion, kindness, humility, gentleness and patience.**
> **Colossians 3:12**

Seven Stone Steps

We live in a world that can be terribly harsh and critical. Hungry people are lazy. The unemployed are shiftless. Addicts are disgusting. Prostitutes are detestable. The old and infirm are inconvenient and uninteresting. Inmates are hopeless. The poor are slothful. The rich are greedy. The talented are proud. Those in authority are arrogant.

In some cases those accusations may partially apply. But in all those cases people need brotherly kindness and often, despite our preconceptions, are examples of brotherly kindness themselves. In the midst of this critical and selfish environment there are always uplifting exceptions.

I have a friend who studied medicine and graduated at the top of his class from medical school and then again from his resident training. He completed a program in one of the most demanding and lucrative fields of medicine and was offered a starting salary near a half million dollars a year. That job went to someone else because my friend elected to move his family to Africa and serve as a missionary doctor where he had to raise his own support and work much longer hours than in a US hospital. He did this because his heart was not focused on what would happen to him if he went but rather what would happen to countless sick and maimed African "brothers" if he didn't. *Philadelphia.*

I have another friend that any airline in the world would be eager to hire. He has a university degree, is certified at the highest levels of commercial piloting and aircraft mechanics, and is fluent in six languages. He has a master's degree in aviation safety administration and thousands of hours of international flying time and mechanical repair experience on four continents.

But all those lucrative airline jobs have been filled by far less qualified people because my friend has chosen to use his multiple impressive skills to provide aviation services in the most needy and dangerous areas of Africa and Asia. He doesn't consider what will happen to him. He constantly considers what will happen to starving, sick, abandoned and isolated people if he doesn't deliver food and medicine on a regular basis. *Philadelphia.*

And since most of us don't have the skills or talents to make such impressive contributions there are countless other areas for brotherly kindness. Soup kitchens, Big Brothers, jail ministries, neighbors, friends, relatives, the poor, the jobless, the homeless, the lonely, the sick, the weak, the dying.

It is what Christ did, and it is through His great and precious promises that we can participate in that divine nature. It is a reasonable response of gratitude for the grace and forgiveness we have been freely given. And because He is God and doesn't need anything, brotherly kindness is our best option. *"I tell you the truth, whatever you did for one of the least of these brothers of mine, you did for me"* (Matthew 25:40).

"For this very reason, make every effort to add to your faith . . . brotherly kindness."

> "Carve your name on hearts and
> not on tombstones."
> -Charles Spurgeon

Now about brotherly love we do not need to write to you, for you yourselves have been taught by God to love each other.
1 Thessalonians 4:9

Chapter Nine

The Step of Love

"Love is the sum of all virtue and love
disposes us to good."
-Jonathan Edwards

**And over all these virtues put on love,
which binds them all together in perfect unity.
Colossians 3:14**

So, in the end, these seven steps of virtue arrive at the terminus named "love." Each has a distinct character of its own, but they each constitute a step up in the Christian life to that inner sanctuary which Peter calls love. (More on that later). It is the spiritual equivalent of the early Jews walking up seven stone steps to the presence of God in the courtyard of the temple. And just as they had to do that over and over, so we must mount those individual steps of goodness, knowledge, self-control, perseverance, godliness and brotherly kindness to arrive (at times) at that most intimate courtyard which Peter describes as love.

But this is a particular love and it is particularly important to understand what Peter is saying because he wrote in a sort of street version of Greek and the word he used was far more meaningful than our simple English word "love".

Greek was a precise language. At the time the New Testament was written there were four different words that could be translated "love" in modern English.

The Greek <u>eros</u> covers everything from queasy stomachs and warm fuzzy feelings to strong sensual passion, including the English derivative "erotic," although eros is not limited to sexual connotation. It is quite well defined by the seven-year-old who said, "When you love somebody, your eyelashes go up and down and little stars come out of you." Good definition of "eros" but that is not the word that Peter uses here.

<u>Storge</u> can be rendered "natural affection" in English and it is most often used to describe family affections. Storge is the natural affection that a parent feels for his or her child or a brother for a sister. Peter does not use "storge" here.

<u>Phileo</u> is the brotherly love that we described in the last chapter. It is a virtuous love that includes loyalty and affection for friends and family. It is the love between close friends. Phileo is one component of a strong marriage relationship, but it is short of the deep and robust love that God desires between spouses. Peter used "phileo" joined with "adelphos" (brother) to describe "brotherly kindness" as the sixth virtue in this list, but for the final, crowning virtue he uses a very different word with a far more intense meaning.

In order to describe this crowning virtue, Peter uses the Greek word <u>agape</u>. *For this very reason add to your faith goodness, knowledge, self-control, perseverance, godliness, brotherly kindness and agape.*

Eros, storge, and phileo are each a sort of response to some outside stimulus. We eros someone or something that elicits powerful emotions. We storge someone with whom we have a warm familial bond. We phileo someone to whom we have grown particularly close and loyal. They are all, to some extent, reactions to outside events.

Agape is not a reaction; it is a decision, a commitment, a promise. It may include all of the first three above, but it is a great leap beyond reactions to an act of the will that obligates us by a determined covenant to proactively seek the well-being of another without regard to their response. Agape is a sacrificial love, including the sacrifice of our own pride and self-interest. Agape is an unconditional love that arises not from a response to some kindness or relationship but from the single, selfless desire to benefit another. Agape is that deep, abiding, committed love that within marriage stimulates the eros and the phileo so that taken all together they turn a bland relationship into the kind of matrimony that God intended from the beginning and that few ever fully experience. It is also the love that God models for us; it is how He loves us and therefore, as Peter says, *"For this very reason, add to your faith . . . agape love."*

> "God is the source of love; Christ is the proof of love; service is the expression of love; boldness is the outcome of love."
> -Henrietta C. Mears

Whoever does not love does not know God, because God is love.
1 John 4:8

It turns out that the Greek word agape was seldom used in classical Greek writing—in the epics and plays and essays that we might read in a classic literature class. Greek heroes and heroines apparently didn't agape one another and Greek philosophers didn't explore that dimension in much depth, if at all.

But agape is used frequently in the New Testament and apparently for a simple reason. Agape is such a selfless and sacrificial love that it is the only way to describe God's love for man and, by extension, the kind of love that man should strive for in all of his relationships. *"Dear friends, let us love one another, for love comes from God"* (1 John 4:7).

Seven Stone Steps

The point is simple. The bar is set very high for any manifestation of agape love because it is the essence of God's love as expressed in His commitment to justify man. Just consider the issue from God's perspective, if that is possible. He created a race of beings whose single purpose was to love Him and enjoy His creation in purity. He gave them only one, clear command, "Don't eat that fruit over there on that tree." Any three year-old would understand that.

And then the man and his woman just couldn't resist the temptation to try it, which they did, and that act introduced sin and rebellion to the world. And in an irreversible process the children continued the rebellion in their own creative ways, and their children, and all children to the present day. Sin had come to stay.

But God wanted some way to deliver those people because He loved them, even as they were, because God is the source of love.

And Christ is the proof of love. It is a proof that begs for some thoughtful consideration because while the cross is the nexus of God's love for mankind, the cross has a long and rich precedent that saturates it with meaning.

> "The cross is God's connection between time and eternity. He planned it from the foundation of the world, and it is intended for the whole world."
> -Richard C. Halverson

When you were dead in your sins . . . God made you alive with Christ. He canceled the written code, with its regulations, and he took it away, nailing it to the cross.
Colossians 2:13-14 (abbreviated)

The cross is God's proof of agape love because it is there that God's righteousness was judicially satisfied. It is the cross where the required penalty for sin was paid and the record was cleared for all those who would believe.

Think of it like this. In the fifteenth and sixteenth centuries in England "whipping boys" were established to take the punishment for a young prince or nobleman's son. They were created because of the idea of the divine right of kings, which stated that kings were appointed by God and implied that no one but the king was worthy of punishing the king's son. The "whipping boy" would receive the penalty that the prince deserved because his father, the king, was often not available, and because he was merciful to his children. But that mercy recognized that a price had to be paid—even if not by the prince himself—because justice demanded a penalty. Justice always demands a penalty.

When God established a covenant relationship with the nation of Israel he established a similar process. Justice demanded a penalty for transgressions but God's mercy and compassion intervened to provide a way that spared His people. The Jews were allowed to transfer their sin to special, sanctified animals—lambs and goats—and then sacrifice those animals in a sacred ritual that drained their blood as the approved means of atoning for the peoples' sin. They didn't have whipping boys but they did have sacrificial animals that satisfied God's inherent demand for justice in all things. Thousands of innocent lambs were executed and their blood shed in order to satisfy God's righteous standard that *"without the shedding of blood there is no forgiveness"* (Hebrews 9:22). Justice always demands a penalty.

But this ritual could not go on forever and there had to be some permanent accommodation that would reconcile God's mercy and His righteous judgment. That resolution involved one final, perfect sacrifice that would forever unite His mercy and His judgment for all men. That was the cross. That was the death of Jesus Christ, *"the lamb of God who takes away the sins of the world"* (John 1:29). That was the perfect expression of "agape," a selfless love that originated without external stimulus and which was thoroughly and passionately directed to the well-being of me, and you, and all who would be willing to believe by faith and not by sight.

At the cross, God altered the very order of the moral universe. He made it possible for all men and women, regardless of their corruption and flaws and rebelliousness and sin to become a part of His family and His kingdom. His motive for doing that was nothing other than agape and that because it is His nature and essence. *"God is love"* and *"God commends His love toward us in that while we were yet sinners Christ died for us"* and *"But God demonstrates his own love for us in this: While we were still sinners, Christ died for us"* (Romans 5:8).

I had an older friend who was fond of describing the meaning of the cross in a unique and abbreviated way. He wanted to express that Jesus Christ was the perfect, sinless Lamb of God who became our whipping boy and paid for our failures. And he equally wanted to express that while we have been forgiven and pronounced righteous in God's judicial view, we live out lives that are never free from transgression. And so my friend was fond of saying this about the cross and those who believed: "There was no sin in Him but our sin was on Him, and now God sees no sin on us but there is still sin in us."

And it is all the consequence of His agape because "the cross is God's connection between time and eternity."

> "We can do no great things; only small
> things with great love."
> -Mother Teresa

And let us consider how we may spur one another on toward love and good deeds.
Hebrews 10:24

So, we are left with the question: What are those small things of love and good deeds? What would it mean to *"add to our faith . . . agape love?* (2 Peter 1:5, 7).

A good illustration of agape love can be found in these imaginary descriptions of two banquets: one in Heaven and one in Hell:

In Hell, people are seated at a lavish dining table covered with gourmet foods of every kind. The food is attractively displayed in bowls in the middle of the table and each person has a very long spoon to reach whatever food he desires. Unfortunately, the spoon is so long that they cannot stretch their arms out sufficiently to maneuver the spoon end to their mouths. So, they sit there in the middle of a sumptuous banquet trying over and over to feed themselves but unable to do so. It is an eternity of tantalizing frustration.

In Heaven, the people are seated at a lavish dining table covered with gourmet foods of every kind. The food is attractively displayed in bowls in the middle of the table and each person has a very long spoon to reach whatever food he desires. But, since this is Heaven, each person uses his spoon to serve another so that the long spoons are a benefit and an opportunity to express love for others. In heaven it is all about the others. Agape.

Agape love always requires denial of self and a love for the other. It is never based on an external motivation, but rather on a personal determination to consider others more important than ourselves. *"Love the Lord your God with all your heart and with all your soul and with all your strength, and love your neighbor as yourself"* (Luke 10:27).

That kind of selfless love contradicts our nature so it requires thoughtful consideration at all times. Incidentally, there is a modern and thoroughly misguided interpretation of that verse which says that in order to love others you must first learn to love yourself more, that you should cultivate agape love for yourself, which is a contradiction in terms because agape always is focused on the other. You do not need to love yourself more. You already love and serve yourself deeply and fervently. But, you can better appropriate and recognize God's love for you, which is a great source of humility, and therefore a sweet motivation to love others. *"Love your neighbor as yourself."*

There once was a young boy who had recovered from a potentially fatal disease because his immune system was able to produce the antibodies it needed to destroy the infection. It seemed like a miracle because the boy eventually recovered to perfect health.

Then his sister contracted the very same disease and despite all of the best medical attention she was declining rapidly. Doctors concluded that her only hope was a blood transfusion from her little brother so that the antibodies in his blood would have a chance to work in her body.

So the parents told the boy that his sister needed his blood in order to live and they wanted him to think about donating it to her.

And because he loved his sister he agreed.

As the nurse prepared to take the boy's blood he asked his mom, "Will I die right away or will it take a while?" He had assumed that he would be giving all of his blood to his sister and that his donation would amount to giving his life for hers.

The Step of Love

His mom's immediate answer was, "No! You won't die at all. You will only be giving a small portion of your blood. People do this all the time and it will not harm your body."

Now, don't miss the larger implication in this story. The boy's mother gave her son the assurance he needed, to know that he was not going to die because of this procedure. But at a deeper level the boy had already died; he had died to himself by being willing to give every drop of his blood to save his sister. Can you imagine that kind of agape love?

It is what Christ did for us and what He longs for us to do for others in common daily actions. Love of others. Sacrificial love. Charity. Benevolence regardless of the price. Agape.

> "Who would have thought that a Lamb
> could rescue the souls of men?
> Almighty infinite Father,
> faithfully loving your own."
> -Eric Wyse & Dawn Rogers

> **You, my brothers, were called to be free. But do not use your freedom to indulge the sinful nature; rather, serve one another in love. The entire law is summed up in a single command: "Love your neighbor as yourself."**
> **Galatians 5:13-14**

> **And now these three remain:
> faith, hope and love.
> But the greatest of these is love.
> 1 Corinthians 13:13**

Chapter Ten

Staying on Track

"I know the power [that] obedience has of
making things easy which seem impossible."
-Saint Teresa

**But the man who looks intently into the perfect
law that gives freedom, and continues to do
this, not forgetting what he has heard, but
doing it—he will be blessed in what he does.
James 1:25**

Obedience has always had a bad reputation—too burdensome, too stifling, too controlling, too demanding. It is difficult to really embrace obedience unless you can see the benefit and that is hard. But spiritual obedience to the virtues God ordains does have benefits as both Saint Theresa and Jesus' brother, James, mention above. According to them, obedience makes impossible things easy and actually imparts a deep and unique form of freedom to the one who is obedient.

But, does obedience really make things easier and establish a sort of freedom? That seems like a contradiction, so in order to better understand the benefits of this biblical obedience, consider the following . . .

In 1917 the Culdoz-Modane railway line in France was the scene of what is probably the worst train accident in history. On December 12 of that year, at the height of World War I, a train carrying French soldiers was returning from the Italian front. During a long descent into the valley outside of Modane, the train derailed and some 800-1000 soldiers were killed in the accident. The fire was so intense that most of the bodies were never identified.

Seven Stone Steps

On June 3, 1998 the German high speed Intercity Express (ICE) train number 884 left Munich on its way to the northern city of Hamburg with several intermediate stops along the way. The ICE trains are ultra-modern creations that look something like jet airplanes without wings and travel over special rail beds at speeds up to 155 mph. They are marvels of engineering and wonderfully smooth, quiet and comfortable.

On the last leg of its journey, and about 80 miles south of Hamburg, one of the wheels malfunctioned initiating a sequence of events that caused the rear of the train to derail with catastrophic consequences. In the colossal crackup that wrecked ICE train number 884, 101 people died and 88 were severely injured. It was the worst accident ever of a high speed train.

On May 10, 2002, British Rail train number 365 derailed as it approached Potter's Bar station. As a result the train slid sideways across the station platform and seven people died.

Trains are reliable, comfortable and efficient means of transportation. I have enjoyed riding trains across the plains, across the Rocky Mountains and across parts of Europe. I grew up next to the tracks in my hometown of Medford, MA, and I like trains.

But trains have an inherent limitation. They are designed to run on steel tracks and when they leave those tracks they inevitably encounter problems and often disasters. So the question here is this, "When is a train most free and easy?" And the answer is simple, "When it is on the tracks."

And the associated question is this, "When is a person most free and easy?" And the biblical answer is, "When his life is firmly established on the controlling, directing, regulating rails of God's wisdom."

> "Man is really free only in God, the
> source of his freedom."
> -Sherwood Eddy

**But the man who looks intently into the perfect
law that gives freedom, and continues to do
this, not forgetting what he has heard, but
doing it—he will be blessed in what he does.
James 1:25**

It is so easy to get this "freedom" thing confused. There is a natural, human tendency to think that genuine freedom consists of unrestrained behavior—doing what I want to do when I want to do it and "doing my own thing." Freedom is too often associated with "no rules" and no restrictions. "Don't tell me what to do!" Freedom!

But, consider . . . One person conducts his life without regard to conventions or rules and lives "free" for a considerable time until his freedom violates civil law and he spends time incarcerated. Another person stays on the rails of basic civil law and never spends time in jail. Which one is really free?

One person lives a life free of dietary and other health restrictions, eats what she wants, doesn't exercise and in mid-life finds herself grossly overweight with diabetes and high blood pressure. And because of those medical issues she is now constrained to limited physical activity, multiple medications and a restricted diet. Another person lives on the rails of a generally healthy diet, moderate exercise and basic weight control. In mid-life she is able to hike, bike, walk and work without pain or serious limitation. Which one is really free?

A third person never attempts to control his anger, bitterness or impatience. He lives free of those constraints and becomes a person of stormy emotions, few friends and alienated family.

Seven Stone Steps

Another person seeks to build a life on the rails of biblical virtue: goodness, knowledge, self-control, perseverance, godliness, brotherly kindness and love. Those rails are confining and they direct his life in ways that he would not otherwise go. He sacrifices a great deal of what popular culture calls "freedom" but this man is free from bitterness and anger. He enjoys family and friends because those virtues are like a sweet aroma in his presence. Which one is really free?

James 1:25 refers to *"the perfect law that gives freedom"* and it is fair to say that James is referring to the entire scope or biblical instruction that can be either detailed and lengthy or brief and broad. The Bible is filled with detailed lists of virtues and they are all meaningful and pleasing to our Father. They are not requirements for a relationship with Him, but rather they are insights into what pleases the One who has already received and adopted those who surrender to His grace.

The Bible also contains two, simple and memorable virtues: *"'Love the Lord your God with all your heart and with all your soul and with all your mind.' and 'Love your neighbor as yourself.'"* Whether you focus on those multiple lists of virtues that are the detailed descriptions of the things that please God, or just on the two broad commands that Jesus gave to the spiritual leaders of His time, you will find a fulfilling and satisfying sense of freedom by those rails of moral and spiritual constraint. It is all *"the perfect law that gives freedom."*

> "May I love His commands as
> well as His promises."
> -Puritan Prayer

This is love for God: to obey his commands. And his commands are not burdensome, for everyone born of God overcomes the world.
1 John 5:3-4

W.C. Fields was a famous comedian and actor 100 years ago. He was a hard-drinking and profane man who appeared to have no appetite for spiritual matters and who professed to hate the holiday of Christmas. W. C. Fields spent the last several weeks of his life in a hospital. When a friend came to visit, he noticed with much surprise that W.C. was reading the Bible. "I'm looking for loopholes," Fields declared.

It is a common thing to do. King Saul looked for loopholes in Samuel's instruction to *"Attack the Amalekites and totally destroy everything that belongs to them"* (1 Samuel 15:3). Peter looked for loopholes in God's plan to sacrifice His Son for our sins. Solomon looked for loopholes in God's plan forbidding marriage to pagan women. We all look for loopholes, but when we find them and use them they lead us off the rails of safety and peace.

Jonah ran off the rails in a big way in his pursuit of the freedom to ignore God's personal command to *"Go to the great city of Nineveh and preach against it, because its wickedness has come up before me"* (Jonah 1:2). Jonah couldn't abide with the idea of sharing God's personal message of forgiveness with the hated, cruel and pagan Assyrians. Jonah didn't want the Assyrians to benefit from God's mercy and grace. He wanted them to suffer eternally for their cruelty to Israel.

So he boarded a ship going in the opposite direction, heading to the exciting western frontier where he could expect freedom and excitement. It was doubtless exhilarating to Jonah to feel the sea air as it filled great sails and drove them toward the mysterious boundaries of the known world and away from the odious assignment to evangelize Nineveh. For a moment in time he must have felt free and liberated from the constraints of obedience to the sovereign God. The wind in his hair, the warm breezes of the Mediterranean, the anticipation of something new and exciting. Free, but not free. Not free because he had left the rails of God's will.

Seven Stone Steps

Jonah experienced a sense of freedom for a moment and then sudden confinement in the dark, stinking belly of a really big fish. It is a creative parable of the consequences of any search for freedom off the rails of God's will. It all seems so exhilarating at first and then that apparent freedom of spiritual apathy, drugs, alcohol, deceit, sexual immorality, explosive anger, nurtured bitterness, financial irresponsibility or gossip eventually becomes even more confining than the rails we were seeking to leave. Jonah's short experience of "freedom" brought him to a place of greater confinement than he ever imagined.

There are no loopholes. We are masters at fabricating them but there are no loopholes in God's economy. There are only rails—helpful, guiding, regulating, shepherding rails of protection and safety.

> "The basic test of freedom is perhaps
> less in what we are free to do than
> what we are free not to do."
> -Eric Hoffer

**I will walk about in freedom,
for I have sought out your precepts.
Psalm 119:45**

This is a book about nurturing Christian virtues, using the passage from 2 Peter 1:3-8. It is about cultivating those seven virtues that Peter mentions: *goodness, knowledge, self-control, perseverance, godliness, brotherly kindness and love.*

But the intent here is to encourage an interest in all of the virtues described in the Bible but with two important points of understanding. First, no combination of virtues, no matter how complete or how well-developed can establish us in a personal relationship with God. That can only be accomplished by the atoning work of Jesus Christ on the cross and our personal and humble submission to that sacrifice and to His Lordship over our lives.

Second, it is impossible for anyone to fully develop all of the biblical virtues in this life. We can purpose to identify the rails of Godly living and travel on those rails, but because of our flawed moral nature we will not always succeed. There is no perfect life here. *"If we claim we have not sinned, we make him out to be a liar and his word is not in us"* (1 John 1:10). There is no perfect life here; there is simply more or less commitment to stay on the rails that provide freedom and peace.

And finally, there is that encouraging reassurance that *"If we confess our sins, he is faithful and just and will forgive us our sins and purify us from all unrighteousness"* (1 John 1:9). When we leave the rails, and cause our own train wreck, He is willing and able to repair and forgive. He just requires our humble cooperation.

So as Ezekiel described his vision of seven steps leading up to the inner court of the temple and thus closer to God so we can step up these seven virtues proclaimed by God through His servant Peter. And with some knowledge and effort—and by relying on the power of the Holy Spirit who makes our bodies His temple—we can fold virtually all the hundreds of biblical virtues into those seven: *goodness, knowledge, self-control, perseverance, godliness, brotherly kindness and love.*

> "Obedience is the means whereby we show
> the earnestness of our desire
> to do God's will."
> -Oswald Chambers

Seven Stone Steps

**So let's keep focused on that goal, those of us who want everything God has for us. If any of you have something else in mind, something less than total commitment,
God will clear your blurred vision-
you'll see it yet! Now that we are
on the right track let's stay on it.
Philippians 3:15-16 (The Message)**

About the Author

Dan Manningham has been married to his wife Fran for 53 years. They have 7 children and 28 grandchildren. They are both NANC Certified Biblical Counselors with an active counseling ministry within their church. He is a preaching elder in their local church and occasional speaker at other churches and conferences.

They have served as short term missionaries and/or visited mission fields in Mali (West Africa), Kenya, Tanzania, Papua, Papua New Guinea, Costa Rica and Brazil, and countries in Central Asia.

Dan has served on the Board of Directors at Mission Aviation Fellowship, Mission Safety International, PACTEC, Mansfield Christian School and Richland Pregnancy Services. He is retired after 33 years at United Airlines where his last position was 747 Captain.

Dan has published several hundred articles and three books on aviation safety issues. He is the author of *Six Stone Jars: God's Remedy for Fear, Worry and Anxiety* and *Eight Stone Gates: Taking Thoughts Captive*. He can be contacted by email at stonejars@yahoo.com, or visit his blog at: http://stonebooks.blogspot.com